ScLL	ScCR	ScME	ScWE	ScEp
		11/95	6/03	
ScA	ScHA	ScPA	ScMob	
ScBD	ScKY	ScRD	ScFr	

Angela Sommer-Bodenburg

the little Vampire

AND THE

CHRISTMAS SURPRISE

Translated by Sarah Gibson

Illustrated by Anthony Lewis

SIMON & SCHUSTER
YOUNG BOOKS

This book is for everyone who thinks
the Little Vampire shouldn't
be missing from the nicest evening of the year —
and, of course, for Burghardt Bodenburg too!

Text copyright © 1990 Angela Sommer-Bodenburg
Illustrations copyright © 1994 Anthony Lewis

First published in Germany in 1990 by C. Bertelsmann Verlag GmbH,
under the title *Anton und der Kleine Vampir Fröhliche Weinachten!*

First published in Great Britain in 1994
by Simon & Schuster Young Books
Campus 400
Maylands Avenue
Hemel Hempstead
Herts HP2 7EZ

Set in 12pt Goudy Old Style by
Derek Doyle & Associates, Mold, Clwyd
Printed and bound by the
Guernsey Press Co Ltd, Channel Islands

British Library Cataloguing in Publication Data available

ISBN 0 7500 1539 X
ISBN 0 7500 1540 3 (pb)

Contents

The Story so far...

Tony's best friends – Rudolph and Anna Sackville-Bagg – are vampires! They live with their creepy Aunt Dorothy and their teenage brother, Greg, in the family vault in the cemetery.

Tony's parents don't believe that vampires really exist, and think that his obsession with these creatures is unhealthy. Little do they know that Tony and Anna are in love, and that his "friends" have really been dead for over a hundred years!

The vampires' main enemies are McRookery – the nightwatchman at the cemetery – and his assistant, Sniveller. Vampires face danger at every turn, and Tony feels responsible for helping his friends to avoid all the perils that await them ...

What Would You Like?

"Tony, telephone!"

Tony heard his mother calling. He knew it had rung, but was hoping the call wasn't for him.

"Coming," he drawled, getting up.

Who could be ringing him at this time of day? If it had been dark, it might have been his best friends, Rudolph, the Little Vampire, or his sister Anna! But now . . .

"It's probably Viola!" thought Tony. Ever since they had come back from the school trip, she had been getting on his nerves, going on and on at him to fix up a meeting between herself and Rudolph. She really thought the Little Vampire was a film star, and believed he could get her a part in his vampire film!

"Hurry up!" said Tony's mother, as he wandered slowly across the hall. "Or do you want Granny to get a huge phone bill?"

"Oh, it's Granny, is it?" Tony was at the telephone in a few strides. After the usual questions, like "How was he?" and "What was he doing in school?" Tony's grandmother came out with the real reason for her call. "I wanted to talk to you about Christmas."

"About Christmas?" repeated Tony.

"Yes, Grandpa and I want to know what you would like."

"Hmmm . . ." Tony hesitated. It wouldn't do to answer too quickly.

"It's – it's a bit sudden," he said.

"I do hope you aren't going to ask for any silly things again," Granny remarked.

"Silly things? I don't know what you're talking about," said Tony, all innocence.

"Don't you?" she said. "Last year you made up an impossible list of things you wanted . . ."

"Impossible?" Tony chuckled to himself. "Coffins are normal, everyday things, aren't they? After all, coffin-maker's a very respectable profession," he added, remembering "John Woodcoat – Grave Furniture".

He could hear his grandmother on the other end of the line, gasping for breath. "Wanting a coffin for Christmas is certainly not a normal, everyday thing to do," she said severely. "And that's why I'm ringing you up especially early – to give you time to think of a few sensible things you might like, that are suitable for your age. Grandpa was wondering if you'd like a pair of ice-skates."

"Ice-skates? He can't have been reading his newspaper!"

"What do you mean?"

"Well, global warming and all that . . . The ponds aren't going to freeze over any more."

"I can see that you're not in the right mood today to talk about Christmas," said Tony's grandmother, sounding a little annoyed. "Just think quietly in your own time about what you might like. Now I'd like another word with your mother."

"Mum, telephone!" called Tony, marching back to his room. He had just sat down at his desk when the door opened and his mother came in.

"Is something the matter, Tony?" she asked.

"What do you mean?" he replied defensively.

"Granny says you don't seem to be looking forward to

Christmas one bit!"

"Well, she's right!" said Tony whole-heartedly.

"Why ever not?" his mother wanted to know.

"Because—" Tony looked out of the window, "because I haven't heard anything from Anna or Rudolph for so long," he admitted finally.

The Little Vampire had only paid him one visit since the school trip, and even Anna had only come to see him once, to pick up Uncle Theodore's cloak. Her grandparents, Sabina the Sinister and William the Wild, wanted to collect all the family's cloaks together to wash and mend them, Anna had told him.

But Tony's mum didn't need to know that.

"So now you're worried about them, are you?" she demanded.

"No, not exactly," he said evasively.

"What if we were to invite them round at Christmas?" Mum suggested.

"What?" exclaimed Tony.

"Not for Christmas Eve, of course," she went on. "I'm sure Anna and Rudolph will want to spend that time with their family. Or don't you think they celebrate it at all?" she asked, after a pause.

"Well, they certainly don't celebrate in the same way as us."

"Well then, if they're not doing anything special at home, of course Anna and Rudolph could come and spend Christmas Eve with us. Although, personally, I'd prefer them to come on Boxing Day . . ."

Tony's mother gave an awkward laugh. As Christmas was the festival of goodwill, she was obviously embarrassed that she didn't particularly like his friends!

"Will you invite them then?" she asked, when he gave no reply.

9

"Yes," he muttered.

"You've got their telephone number, haven't you?" she asked, watching him carefully.

Tony gave a start. "Their telephone number?"

"If you want, I could ring them up!"

"No, no," Tony said hastily, "I'd like to invite them myself."

"When?" asked Mum.

"As soon as possible."

A Nice Little Place

However, just as Tony had expected, that evening and the next few passed without either Anna or the Little Vampire knocking on his window.

At last Saturday arrived – the evening when his parents usually went out.

"Haven't you asked Anna and Rudolph yet?" asked Tony's mum, appearing in Tony's doorway wearing her tight black suit.

"No," he said.

"Why not?"

Tony rolled his eyes. "Because I haven't seen them."

"But you were going to ring them up!"

"Yeah . . ."

"Well?"

Tony found it difficult to keep a straight face. "There was no answer."

It wasn't even a lie, as there was no telephone in the Sackville-Bagg vault!

"Then you must try again!" said his mother. "After all, it's the ninth of December already. I'd like to be prepared, if we're going to have guests at Christmas – and anyway, we'll have to get presents for Rudolph and Anna, if they do come."

"Yes, *if* they come," said Tony with a sigh.

After his parents had gone, he switched on the TV in his bedroom. Tony's parents had had it repaired at long last, after weeks and weeks. Actually, they needn't have bothered, when you saw what was on that evening: he had the choice of "The Jolly Village Warblers", a poor Western on its tenth or eleventh repeat broadcast, or a "cultural" programme with four ancient men and one woman sitting around in leather armchairs arguing about boring books.

Tony decided to do some more drawing on the calendar he was going to give his parents for Christmas. There was a different page for every month and he had already filled two pages with "Scenes from the life of a vampire". He was looking forward to his parents' reaction when they saw the drawings. In January, there was a picture of three vampires having a snowball fight and in February, vampires were tossing pancakes at a pancake party. Tony was still working on the picture for March. It was going to be something to do with vampires and Spring.

As he was sharpening his crayons, he suddenly heard a noise at the window. It sounded as though horribly long fingernails were scraping down the glass in slow motion.

Tony's hair stood on end. If only he had closed the curtains! Right now, by the light of his desk-top lamp, the vampire outside – and he was quite sure it was neither Rudolph nor Anna – could see him as clearly as if he were on a brightly lit stage!

What if it were Aunt Dorothy . . .?

Tony stared at the black rectangle of window, hoping to see who was lurking outside. Then he heard a voice that sounded at first squeaky, and then deep and gravelly. "Hey, did that noise go in one ear and out the other? Or have you grown to be part of your desk?" it said. It was Gruesome Gregory, the Little Vampire's elder brother!

At first Tony was rather relieved, but almost immediately he began to feel uneasy. It couldn't be anything good that had brought Greg of all people to visit him!

Knees knocking, Tony went over to the window and opened it.

"You've got a nice little place here, haven't you? I don't suppose anyone ever disturbs you, do they?" asked Greg, with a suspicious glance at the door.

Tony nodded, thinking Unfortunately they do!

"Well then!" Grinning happily, Greg jumped down into the room. The wave of 'perfume' that came in with him nearly took Tony's breath away. It was a powerful smell of decay, mixed with some sort of sharp, antiseptic smell, like there is at the doctor's.

"Yes, yes," Greg was saying genially. "This time it's worked!"

"Worked?"

"Yes. Haven't you noticed anything?"

"No . . ." Whatever happened, Tony didn't want to say the wrong thing and upset Greg.

"Use your eyes!" chuckled Greg, turning Tony's desk-top lamp so that the light shone on his chin. "What about now?"

"Your skin . . ."

"Brilliant, isn't it?" Greg was grinning like the Cheshire cat. "Connections, Tony Peasbody – in the end it all comes down to connections!"

"Connections?"

"Yes! Cultivate the people you know, and you'll go a long way in life!"

In "life"? Now it was Tony's turn to grin.

Greg continued, hissing angrily, "The few remaining spots will soon disappear, Sniveller says. His 'Pimple-

Clear' is a miraculous lotion, you know!"

"Sniveller gave you a lotion?" Tony was amazed. "What did McRookery have to say about that?" The Nightwatchman at the cemetery wouldn't be at all pleased to find that Sniveller had been helping a vampire with a skin problem!

"McRookery? He's still in bed!" retorted Greg.

"Still in bed?" repeated Tony.

"Well, most of the time," Greg admitted. "McRookery hasn't been the same at all since his heart attack, Sniveller says. He's even thinking of changing jobs!"

"McRookery's going to change jobs?"

"No!" Greg tapped a finger on Tony's forehead. "You really aren't very bright today, are you! *Sniveller*'s thinking of changing jobs. He's toying with the idea of retraining as a hairdresser. Actually, it wouldn't be such a bad thing, as far as I'm concerned. He just wouldn't be able to put up any mirrors in his salon, ha, ha!"

Dumbfounded

Greg continued, suddenly serious again, "If Sniveller didn't have me, he would have left long ago. He says it's only our night-time conversations in the cemetery that keep him here."

"But wouldn't it be better for your family if Sniveller did go?" Tony remarked cautiously. "I mean, then you'd have one less enemy."

Greg laughed harshly. "It's not just dim inside your pea-brain – it's pitch black!"

"That's what you think, is it?" asked Tony coolly.

"Sure do! McRookery with Sniveller to help him is far less dangerous for us than McRookery *without* him!"

"Hmm, I suppose you could look at it that way . . ."

"It's not just me! The whole Family Council sees it like that," boasted Greg.

"The Family Council?" Tony repeated, surprised.

Greg drew himself up. "The Family Council has authorized me, Gruesome Gregory, to cultivate my connection with Sniveller in the interests of the entire family! That's got you dumbfounded, hasn't it?" he asked, looking at Tony as though he expected applause.

"It certainly has!" said Tony.

"Yes," Greg smiled conceitedly. "My first good deed is to take part in the Christmas celebrations in McRookery's house!"

"You're going to *what?*" exclaimed Tony.

"You heard me!" Greg giggled. "Sniveller has invited me to celebrate Christmas with McRookery and himself. I'm going to accept his invitation – only because it's in our family's interests for me to do so, naturally!"

Tony could hardly believe his ears. "You *want* to celebrate Christmas with McRookery?"

"Why not?" said Greg. "If I make myself a bit more presentable . . ." He tugged at his blond, matted hair. "I shall have a Christmas haircut, put on a bit of Aunt Dorothy's make-up . . ."

Tony pricked up his ears. "Aunt Dorothy? Is she back then?"

Greg looked at him coldly. "Yes. But don't keep sidetracking me with stupid questions. Now then, where were we . . .? Oh yes, we were about to talk about *your* contribution to all this."

"My contribution?" murmured Tony with a feeling of foreboding.

"You said it!" Greg bounded over to the door and tore it open.

"First of all, you can give me a tour of your flat and all the Christmas decorations. My eyes have got to start getting used to all these unvampire-like sights."

"But—" Tony began.

"No buts!" thundered Greg. "Or do you want to hinder Gruesome Gregory in the task officially given to him by the Family Council of the Sackville-Baggs!"

"No—"

"Then come along!"

"If you insist . . ." Uneasily, Tony followed Greg out into the hallway.

As he'd guessed, the inspection of the flat turned out to be a disappointment for Gregory. Apart from a couple of holly boughs and an Advent wreath in the kitchen, there was absolutely nothing "Christmassy" to be seen.

Greg shook his head in disbelief. "What about your tree?" he exclaimed. "With all the little balls and candles?"

Tony bit his lip. "It's too early to put that up yet."

"Too early?" growled Greg.

"Yes. Most people only start putting decorations up a few days before Christmas. And we buy our Christmas tree as late as possible, so it doesn't drop needles everywhere. I was going to tell you all this," he added, "but you wouldn't let me get a word in!"

"What a swizzle! What a typical Peasbody swizzle!" cried Greg. "How am I supposed to get used to unvampire-like sights if everything's as dull as ditchwater in your home?"

"You could fly around town and look in all the shopwindows," suggested Tony.

"No, it's not the same thing," Greg grumbled. "It has to be someone's home." He scratched his head thoughtfully.

All of a sudden, he gave a deep, throaty laugh. "I've got it! What do we care what other people do? It doesn't make the slightest difference whether 'people' only start decorating their homes just a few days before Christmas! *You're* going to start decorating now!"

"What if my parents don't agree?" asked Tony.

"Then you'll just have to use your charm on them," Greg told him. "In the same way you use your charm on Anna!"

That was the cue Tony had been waiting for. "How is Anna?" he asked.

"All right," Greg replied evenly. "Why do you ask?"

"Because . . . she hasn't been over here for ages. Nor – nor has Rudolph."

Greg shrugged his shoulders. "Probably got something more important to do."

"But I've got an invitation for them," Tony cleared his throat. "My parents want them to celebrate Christmas with us."

"How touching," said Greg. "But I don't think they'll come."

"Why not?"

"Because unlike me, they haven't been instructed to do so by the Family Council. It's hardly in our family's interests for them to come and spend Christmas with Tony Peasbody."

Tony grimaced. "It might be in Anna and Rudolph's interests though," he insisted.

"Well, all right, I'll pass on the invitation," Greg offered grudgingly. "Of course, only because *I'm* already fixed up for Christmas." He giggled. "Otherwise I'd come and pay you all a visit too!"

Striding over to the living room window, he opened it, without paying any attention to the two potted plants on the sill. The pots fell to the ground with a crash, but luckily stayed in one piece.

Greg turned and grinned. "You'd better start on the decorations," he said, "otherwise you won't have finished when I come back tomorrow evening!"

"First I'll have to sweep up all this soil!" retorted Tony crossly.

"Have fun!" chuckled Greg, and swung off out into the night.

The Christmas Tree

At first, Tony thought he was still dreaming when he opened his eyes next morning and saw a tree-shaped horror standing in the middle of his room. Then he remembered that, at some time during the night, there had been a tap on his window. Half asleep, he had groped his way over to the window, and with the words, "Here! This one's guaranteed not to drop its needles!" Greg had thrown this green monstrosity into the room and had flown away.

Tony looked at the "tree" with distaste. It looked too unrealistic for words. The whole thing – right down to the balls, the little bells and the angel on the top – was made out of plastic!

Tony sighed. He could just imagine what his mother was going to say about this horror of a Christmas tree. "That thing belongs on the rubbish tip – in fact, on the hazardous waste tip!" she'd say. And she would be quite right, Tony thought.

If Greg hadn't promised to come back that evening, Tony would have dumped the plastic monstrosity in the basement ready for the next dustbin collection! But in the circumstances, there was nothing for him to do but set up Greg's "Christmas tree" in the flat.

Later, when he was sitting at breakfast with his parents, Tony steered the conversation casually in the right direction.

"Now I'm beginning to look forward to Christmas," he said.

"Ah! Have you managed to talk to Anna and Rudolph then?" asked his mother.

"No," he replied. "I mean I've started to get in the mood. There's just one thing I'm not happy about."

"What's that then?" Dad wanted to know.

Tony took a sip of hot chocolate. "Well, it's the Christmas tree. I don't think we should buy a real tree this year."

His father laughed. "But a real tree is what Christmas is all about!"

"What about the destruction of the forests?" said Tony. "Don't you ever think about that?"

"What's the destruction of the forests got to do with our Christmas tree?" asked Mum.

"Because at Christmas time, whole forests are cut down!" Tony said dramatically.

"Yes, but only trees that were planted especially for Christmas," retorted his mother. "They've got nothing to do with the destruction of the forests. After all, we're not going to buy an oak or a beech tree," she added.

Tony pressed his lips together. It looked as though he was going to have to tackle the problem himself and put up Greg's ghastly tree in his own bedroom!

There was still another problem. "Couldn't we put up the decorations a bit earlier this year?" he asked. "After all, today's the second Sunday of Advent already!"

"We deliberately haven't started yet because you complained so much last year!" Mum explained. "Don't you remember how I wanted to make the bathroom look a bit more festive and put up a little crib in it? You moaned and moaned until I took it down!"

"I only moaned because the sheep and the donkey

were always falling over," said Tony.

"Well, I think it's a good idea," Tony's father put in. "After all, it's nice to get into the spirit of Christmas early."

"Why this sudden change of heart?" Mum demanded, giving Tony a searching look.

Tony grinned. He could hardly admit that Greg was behind his "change of heart". "Well," he said craftily, "perhaps I'll get more presents this way . . ."

"Up to your tricks, are you?" laughed Dad.

"Typical Tony!" said Mum, looking peeved. "As if Christmas was simply a time for presents!"

"A time for the right presents!" Tony corrected her. "You might like to know that my list is nearly finished."

"Well, we can't wait to see it!" Mum said with a touch of sarcasm. She was obviously thinking about last year, when Tony's list had included a coffin, a vampire cloak, black sheets and pillowcases for his bed, black candles and a set of false vampire teeth from the dentist.

"We'll start decorating the flat after lunch," Tony's father said, rubbing his hands together enthusiastically. "Will you help me bring up the box of Christmas things from the basement, Tony?"

"Of course!" said Tony happily.

By the evening, angels of all sizes, Father Christmases, stars, balls and little bells were hanging all over the place, even in the bathroom.

"You haven't left anything to go on the tree," said Mum doubtfully. She had been marking school work in her room and hadn't taken part in the decorating.

"We can buy more things for the tree," replied Dad.

"That's right!" Tony agreed. "You can get really funny things this year."

"Funny?" His mother raised her eyebrows. "I suppose

you mean little vampires in cloaks, and bells in the shape of coffins!"

Tony grinned. "No, not yet, unfortunately!"

In fact, he was very pleased with how the flat looked. Now he could look forward to Greg's visit in a fairly relaxed frame of mind. All that was left to do was to set up the revolting plastic tree in his room . . .

"I'm going to my bedroom," he announced. "I want to make something for Christmas."

"Make something?" His mother sounded very pleased. "What a good idea!"

Tony really did have some construction work to do! The monstrous tree had four pieces of wire wrapped round with green insulating tape for "feet", and it took him at least a quarter of an hour to bend them in such a way that the tree wouldn't tip over.

At last he managed it. There stood the tree, sparkling tackily in the middle of the room, its uneven branches jutting out laden with plastic baubles.

Tony sighed. He lay down on his bed and opened his latest book, *Vampires by Themselves*. Any minute now, his mother would be bound to come in and then there would be an almighty scene: Where on earth had he got that tree? How did he dare to bring such an appalling object home? and so on, and so on . . .

December Nights
Are Long

Tony must have fallen asleep over his book, because suddenly it was dark in his room.

He switched on the light. The first thing he saw was the dreadful tree. Almost at once he noticed that his curtains had been drawn. His parents must have done that, so they must have seen the plastic tree . . .

Tony glanced at his watch. It was almost midnight. Were his parents asleep already? He went to the door, opened it a crack and listened. Everything was deathly quiet in the flat – in fact, there was no sound to be heard anywhere in the building.

Suddenly, in the silence, Tony heard someone knocking at his window. At first, he stood rooted to the spot in fright. Then he quickly closed the door and ran over to the window. No way must Greg be kept waiting, because he was quite capable of breaking the window pane!

But it wasn't Greg sitting outside on the window sill . . .

"Rudolph!" exclaimed Tony in a mixture of surprise and delight.

"Hallo, Tony!" said the Little Vampire in his husky voice, and without waiting to be asked, he climbed down into the room.

An extraordinary smell accompanied the vampire – rather like the smell in chemistry lessons, Tony thought.

Was it something to do with the vampire cloaks having been cleaned? Rudolph's cloak looked as though someone had given it a thoroughly good brush or even a wash. All the holes had been darned, and very neatly too.

"Yes, that's got to do me for the next twenty years," said the Little Vampire, noticing Tony's look. Grinning broadly, he pointed to the plastic tree and remarked, "So you've got one too!"

"Greg brought it for me."

The Little Vampire tapped his forehead. "He must have discovered a nest of them somewhere."

"A nest?"

"Yes! A nest of Christmas trees. We've got nine of them at home in the vault!"

"Nine of these plastic Christmas trees?"

"One for each of us. Just imagine! Greg brought them last night. He's supposed to be going to celebrate Christmas with McRookery and Sniveller."

"I know," Tony said.

The Little Vampire looked at Tony suspiciously. "Did Anna tell you?"

"No, Greg told me, before he brought the tree. We've been decorating the entire flat today," Tony went on, "just so he'll have a chance to get used to the sights of Christmas."

"What's that?" The vampire's eyes had narrowed to slits. "Have you let your parents in on it?"

"Of course not!" Tony assured him. "I told them I'd like to put decorations up to get in the mood. Actually, my parents would like to invite you and Anna to celebrate Christmas here with us."

"You want us to come and celebrate Christmas with you?" The idea seemed to please the Little Vampire, for

25

he gave a satisfied smile. "Will we get proper presents if we do?" he went on, glancing over at Tony's bookshelves. "Some exciting stories?"

Tony nodded. "That's why Mum wants to know if you'll come – so she has time to buy something."

"Hmm . . ." The Little Vampire clicked his pointed teeth together. "It would be my first Christmas party in over a hundred and fifty years . . ."

"Does that mean you accept the invitation?" asked Tony.

"No!" spat the Little Vampire. "I'll have to think the whole thing through extremely thoroughly – and I'll have to talk to Anna as well."

"What shall I tell Mum?"

"Your mother?"

"Yes. Should she go ahead and buy presents or not?"

Rudolph gave a husky laugh. "Of course she should buy presents! Even if we don't come and celebrate with you, we could still pick up the presents!"

"How long will you take to think about it?"

"How long?" The Little Vampire raised his eyes to the ceiling. "Could take some time . . ."

"I hope not till the twenty-seventh!" teased Tony.

"Why not? What's so special about the twenty-seventh?" asked the Little Vampire, sounding irritated.

Tony tried hard not to laugh. "Because Christmas is over by 27th December!"

"Oh, that's what you mean!" The Little Vampire had turned red. To cover up his embarrassment, he hissed, "Why didn't you invite us earlier? Then at least I would have had time to think it all through without this rush!"

"For a start, I did ask Greg to pass the invitation on to you both," Tony told him.

"You needn't have bothered," the Little Vampire

interrupted him. "Greg's got a memory like a sieve. What's more, he never does anything for anyone else."

"And secondly," Tony continued, "my parents only suggested we invite you a couple of days ago."

"All right then, I'll think it over and let you know by next Saturday," declared the Little Vampire, sounding pacified. He glanced over at the window. "Now I must be off," he murmured.

"Why did you come over in the first place?" asked Tony.

Turning to face him, the Little Vampire grinned so that Tony could see his gleaming white pointed teeth.

"Can't you guess?" he asked softly.

Tony took a step backwards. "No, I can't," he answered, trying hard to make his voice sound firm and unruffled.

Rudolph giggled. "Just a little joke!" he said. With a lightning movement, he snatched up Tony's book, *Vampires by Themselves*, and tucked it under his cloak. "That's just the sort of thing I like to read. These December nights are long, you know!"

"Hey, I've only just started that!" Tony protested, but the Little Vampire had already flown out of the window.

Tony glared after him. He hadn't even got round to asking Rudolph about Greg!

Once the Little Vampire had faded to a dim and distant shadow in the sky, Tony closed the window, undressed and climbed into bed.

A Real Sensation

Greg never appeared that night.

The next morning, Tony found himself alone in the flat. His father always liked to be "up with the lark", as he put it, and on Mondays Mum had to be at school before eight o'clock, but Tony didn't have to get in till nine. Luckily! he thought to himself. Otherwise his parents would probably have started asking him about the plastic Christmas tree at breakfast. Now at least the trouble could be put off till lunch time . . .

And trouble it was! When Tony got home just after one o'clock, his mother was standing in front of the oven with a grim expression on her face, and it wasn't just because she didn't like cooking!

"Have a look on the table!" she snapped.

"On the table?" The newspaper was lying there.

"Have a good look!"

Tony peered uneasily at the newspaper. It was the *Northern Echo*, a local paper which reported on neighbourhood events, from meetings of the pigeon fanciers, through the Fire Service Annual Ball, to golden and diamond wedding anniversaries.

This time, however, the reporter seemed to have stumbled across a real sensation. MYSTERIOUS ROBBERY the paper proclaimed in bold black letters on the front page.

Under the headline was the photograph of a

department store. No, you could only see the *roof* of the store, Tony realized. A "mysterious robbery" from the roof? What on earth could anyone pinch from up there? He bent over the paper to read the small print.

"You can read it out loud if you like!" commanded his mother.

Tony began. " '11th December. Since Sunday, detectives have been investigating a most mysterious robbery. On Saturday night, ten artificial Christmas trees were—' " Tony hesitated and stole a glance at his mother. She was watching him – unusually critically, he thought.

" ' —ten artificial Christmas trees were stolen from the roof of this department store,' " he read on. " 'The circumstances surrounding the theft are particularly puzzling: the ten trees were taken from the roof of the store, but the heavy iron door which opens on to the roof was locked. It hadn't even been forced, as store manager Mr Harry Clamp (43) confirmed when we asked him. How then did the thieves get on to the roof? Were they cat burglars? Did they have ladders? No evidence has been found to point to which method they might have used.

" 'In the opinion of Detective Inspector Alfred Smallbone (44), it was possible that the thieves might have used a helicopter. But who would go to such trouble just to steal ten artificial Christmas trees?

" 'There is also uncertainty over the motive. Was it carried out by fanatics wanting to protest against the celebration of Christmas by stealing the trees? If so, this mysterious robbery will only be the beginning, and we must prepare ourselves for a series of similar strikes. We can only hope it turns out to be nothing more than a silly practical joke carried out by young hooligans!' "

With these words, the article ended.

Vampires Celebrating Christmas...

Tony felt his ears going red.

"Well?" asked his mother. "Haven't you got anything to say?"

"What should I have to say?" Tony said, all innocence. He felt completely at a loss and couldn't think up even the most feeble excuse.

"What about that frightful fake tree in your bedroom?" Her eyes were searching him. "That isn't a figment of my imagination, is it?"

"No," Tony confirmed, adding to himself, unfortunately!

"It's true, isn't it, that this artificial tree first appeared in your room on Sunday?" his mother demanded.

"Yes."

"If you don't mind telling me, how did it get there?"

Tony hesitated. Should he say that he had simply "found" the tree somewhere? His mum would never believe that, so he replied with the truth. "Greg brought it here," he murmured.

His mother looked at him, puzzled. "Greg? Who or what is Greg?"

"Anna and Rudolph's elder brother. I've told you about him before."

"He brought you the fake tree?"

"Yes."

"When?"

"When?" repeated Tony, stalling for time. "On Saturday. When you were out at the theatre."

"Do you mean to say that you invite people round to the flat late at night when we aren't here?" exclaimed his mother.

"No, no I don't!" Tony retorted quickly. "Greg just dropped in. And I didn't want that horrible tree either," he added.

"Then it would be best if you gave the tree back to Greg," Mum proposed. "I don't want *you* mixed up in this business, on any account! After all, the police are making enquiries already!"

"I *can't* give the tree back to Greg!"

"Why not?"

"Because it was a present. Greg gets terribly angry if you refuse his presents!"

"Hmm . . ." Tony's mother was thinking. "Perhaps Dad and I ought to talk to Greg. Then we could make it clear to him that it was a very, very stupid prank to carry out."

"That's true!" Tony agreed.

"When will you be seeing him again?"

"Probably to– today, sometime." Tony just stopped himself from saying "tonight"!

"But you don't know exactly what time?"

"No. Nothing's ever 'exact' with Greg."

"What about Anna and Rudolph?" inquired Mum. "Do you know anything more exact about them?"

"What – what do you mean?"

"Whether they're going to come over at Christmas or not?"

"Oh, I see . . . Rudolph will have made up his mind by Saturday."

"What about Greg? Perhaps he'd like to come along

too?"

"No, I'm sure he wouldn't!" Tony assured her hastily.

"But if his parents don't celebrate Christmas at home at all . . ." Mum objected.

"He – he's already got something planned. With his gang."

"His gang? He's not one of these young hoodlums who think they're so tough, is he?"

"No." Tony found it hard to keep a straight face. "Greg doesn't just *think* he's tough, he *is* incredibly tough. He's known as Gruesome Gregory the Strong!"

"He's obviously not just incredibly tough," remarked Tony's mum in a slightly mocking tone. "He seems to be an incredibly talented climber as well. How else did he manage to get to those Christmas trees?"

Tony bit his tongue. "I wasn't there to see . . ."

"I suppose he had a helicopter!"

Now Tony had to grin. "No, he didn't have a helicopter." He paused. "But I bet he did . . . fly!"

"Oh really?" She didn't seem at all convinced.

"Yes. He uses his cloak – his *vampire* cloak." As Tony had known, his mother was never going to believe the truth!

"Aha!" was all she said. "You obviously haven't been studying those horror stories of yours particularly thoroughly!"

"What do you mean?"

"Vampires celebrating Christmas?" She laughed drily. "That's about as likely as vampires lying on a sunbed sucking garlic pills!"

"That's what you think!" said Tony.

"Anyhow," she winked at him, "you're surely not trying to persuade me that Greg's a vampire?"

"No, no," Tony assured her. It wasn't a lie, either – he

33

certainly didn't want to persuade her!

"When's lunch?" he asked, deliberately changing the subject.

"Now!" replied Mum, plonking his bowl on the table so that the soup nearly spilled over the edge.

Aunt Dorothy, for Instance

Tony's mother didn't mention the plastic tree again until early evening. Only as it began to get dark did she ask, "Where's Greg got to, then?"

Tony peered out of the kitchen window. "I wish I knew," he said.

Of course, he did know where Greg was – in his coffin! He was probably pushing the heavy lid aside at that very moment, yawning and stretching.

"Do you think he's still going to come?" asked Mum.

"I hope so."

"Why don't you go over to his house?" she suggested. "I don't like you wandering about outside after dark, I know, but under these circumstances . . . Just imagine – if the police are on to Greg's tracks, that might have the most terrible consequences for the rest of his life."

"Life?" Tony grinned. But his mum was probably right. Judging by the stir that the robbery of the artificial trees had caused, it was all too possible that Greg was in trouble.

"Mmm, you're right," said Tony. "I'll bike over to him."

"Shall I come with you?" his mum offered.

"Come with me? No, thanks! Mr Crustscrubber always says, 'If you make your bed, you must lie on it!' "

Mr Crustscrubber was the psychologist who had

35

"clever" conversations with Tony and his parents on more than one occasion.

"All right then," said Tony's mother. "But promise me you'll go straight to Greg's house. Don't stop and hang about anywhere and come straight back home again afterwards."

"OK," he agreed.

Once outside, Tony got on his bicycle and rode off. The shops were still open, so there were quite a few people on the streets, but he didn't meet anyone he knew and reached the cemetery without mishap.

He leant his bike against the white-painted wall behind a medium-sized bush, and approached the entrance gates warily. A sign by the wall read: "In Winter, the cemetery is open until dusk". Perhaps he'd be lucky, and the gates would still be unlocked.

That evening, Tony didn't feel in the least like creeping along the cemetery wall until he found a place where he could climb over – he would much rather use the official paths. He didn't know who to be most afraid of at this early hour of evening: McRookery and his assistant, Sniveller, or the adult vampires. Having only just woken up, they would surely still be hovering around here!

He was lucky: the gates were not locked. Heart beating fast, Tony stepped into the cemetery. The lights along the main pathway were glowing, but otherwise all was dark.

Tony turned left. Even if it was rather a detour, he thought it wise not to go straight past the chapel today. The old emergency exit from the vault came out in the well near the chapel, and for all he knew, one of the vampires might still use it from time to time – Aunt Dorothy, for instance . . .

Tony realized he was getting goosepimples. He tiptoed along, anxious not to make a sound. Vampires have very good ears!

About fifty metres away, on the left-hand side, Tony could now make out McRookery's house. He paused and peered through the hedge, which was almost bare. There was a light on in the hall and two other windows on the ground floor were lit up as well. For a moment, he was tempted to creep up to the house and peep inside. Perhaps McRookery and Sniveller had put up their Christmas decorations too.

He quickly rejected the idea. With the reassuring thought that at least he would be spared a meeting with Sniveller and McRookery, he went on his way.

Soon he came to the old, overgrown part of the cemetery. Pressing himself into the shadows of the trees, he crept over to an evergreen hedge. From here, he could see the great yew tree under which lay the entrance hole to the Sackville-Bagg family vault, well disguised with broken branches and clumps of moss. Tony's plan was to stand and wait until someone came out of the vault. If he were very lucky, it might even be Greg himself!

Suddenly Tony heard distant voices coming from the direction of McRookery's house. He had obviously relaxed too soon! He ducked down. The voices were coming nearer, and now he could hear what they were saying.

"Have you no pity?" That was Sniveller.

"Pooh! Pity!" answered McRookery gruffly. "I don't let myself have such wishy-washy feelings! After all, I'm the Nightwatchman, not a nurse!"

"But my foot! I can hardly walk on it!" whimpered Sniveller.

"All because of a tiny verucca!" said McRookery

scornfully. "Pull yourself together and be quiet, for goodness' sake! Or do you want a vampire to come and bite you?"

"No!" cried Sniveller in fright.

"You see?" said McRookery. "Now come along! Tonight we're going to inspect the old chapel. I've got a funny feeling about that place . . ."

"But the doctor—" Sniveller began.

"The doctor!" McRookery interrupted rudely. "You ought to change jobs if you want to go running to a doctor just because of a teeny-tiny verucca!"

"You don't understand!" wailed Sniveller. "It was *your* doctor in the hospital who said that on no account should you be running around the cemetery at night!"

"So what?" hissed McRookery. "How does that help? Will that get rid of any vampires, huh? That doctor should try saying the same thing to them!"

"Think of your heart – you mustn't get over-excited!" Sniveller implored him. McRookery didn't reply.

Tony lifted his head. He saw McRookery turn and march straight up to the old chapel, followed by a limping Sniveller. He gave a sigh of relief. Then someone tapped him on the shoulder from behind.

He spun round as if he had been given an electric shock.

I Missed You

It was Anna!

"Hallo, Tony!" she said.

"McRookery – he's here!" Tony cried, peering anxiously in the direction of the chapel. He heard a husky cough. Then a lock squeaked and a door closed with a creak.

"And now he's gone into the chapel!" Anna giggled.

"Wh-where have you come from?" asked Tony. It wasn't very original, but nothing better occurred to him.

"Where do you think I've come from?" said Anna with a sigh. "But what are *you* doing here?" she asked.

"Me?" Tony hesitated. He realized it would be best not to come out with the truth straight away! "I wanted to see you again," he declared.

"Really?" Anna was flattered.

"Yes, because . . . we haven't seen each other for such a long time."

"I know," she said softly. "But I wanted to find out if you'd notice."

"Whether I'd notice *what?*"

"That we hadn't seen each other for ages – whether you missed me!"

"I did miss you!" Tony assured her. "I waited for you every evening." That was a bit of an exaggeration, but it was just what Anna wanted to hear!

"Oh, Tony!" she whispered with feeling. "When you

say something like that, I regret every minute I'm not with you . . ."

Tony felt his face going red.

"I wanted to invite you over," he began, quickly changing the subject to a less risky topic.

"Invite me over?"

"Yes, at Christmas. My parents would like you to come and celebrate Christmas with us."

"Really?"

"Yes. I've already told Rudolph about it."

"Why Rudolph? What's he got to do with it?"

"You're both invited. Didn't he tell you?"

"No!" she answered grimly. "He was probably planning to come by himself."

"I can't believe that!" Tony leapt to the Little Vampire's defence. "Rudolph probably hasn't had a chance to tell you about it yet."

"Hasn't he?" Anna shook her fists. "Just now, we were the last two in the vault! He had at least a quarter of an hour then to tell me about it!"

"The last two?" repeated Tony. "Then . . . then Greg's not there any more?"

"He flew off first. To his stupid Men's Music Club!"

"I'm sure Rudolph just forgot," said Tony. "In any case, he's not going to let me know until Saturday."

Anna smiled tenderly. "You've got one acceptance already – mine. I'll come! But now I must fly," she said in quite a different tone of voice, looking round restlessly.

"We could go somewhere else," suggested Tony, who thought she was frightened of the Nightwatchman.

"No." Anna shook her head regretfully. "It's . . . it's . . . well, you know . . ." She stopped and giggled, and then Tony saw her canine teeth, which by now were almost as long and pointed as Rudolph's.

An icy shudder ran over him. "I see . . ." he murmured.

"Shall I come home with you?" she asked.

"B-better not," said Tony hastily. "I've got my bike outside, leaning against the cemetery wall."

"See you soon, then!" She gave him a secret smile, then rose into the air and flew away.

At that very moment, Tony heard the door of the chapel open with a horrible squeak. He made himself as small as he could.

"Nice vampires they turned out to be!" he heard Sniveller say. "I never knew that vampires had four paws and a pointy nose!"

"Pooh! I know exactly what rats look like, thank you!" retorted McRookery angrily.

"And all because of two rats, we've got to clear up the whole chapel tomorrow morning!" Sniveller complained.

"We?" McRookery gave a menacing laugh. "You'll be doing the clearing-up! After all, you're the assistant gardener!"

"But you were the one who threw my rakes and spades all over the place," whined Sniveller.

"Yes! Because it's my confounded duty to follow up the tiniest clue – Aagh!" McRookery suddenly groaned out loud.

"Henry!" cried Sniveller, horrified. "Is it your heart?"

"No," said McRookery sullenly, "my back. O-oh! I think I shall have to go and lie down."

"Here, lean on me!" exclaimed Sniveller.

"On you?" replied McRookery. "How can I lean on you when you're limping so badly?"

"I'm limping because my verucca hurts," Sniveller told him. "But you never believed me."

Tony craned his neck. He could just see McRookery leaning on the arm of a pathetically hobbling Sniveller. They looked like a couple out of a comedy film. He waited impatiently till the two of them had vanished down the path that led to McRookery's house.

Then he ran to the gates of the cemetery. They were still open. He swung himself on to his bike and rode away.

Caught!

Tony had hardly set foot back in the flat when his mother asked, "Did you see Greg?"

"He'd gone out," he replied. "But I met Anna. She's accepted the invitation."

"And Rudolph?"

"He – er – he still hasn't decided."

His mother looked at him in surprise and dissatisfaction. "I must say, I don't think that's very polite of Rudolph!"

"Rudolph's never polite," Tony told her. "But I bet he'll come, even if only because of Anna. He's pretty jealous, you know."

"When are they coming?"

"When?"

"Yes. Which day?"

"Ah, I see . . ." He hadn't discussed that with Anna.

"Christmas Eve," he said, on the spur of the moment.

Tony's mother made a none-too-enthusiastic face. "I would have preferred them to come on Boxing Day. Oh, well. Aren't their family going to celebrate Christmas at all?"

"No, only Greg – he'll be with his gang."

She shook her head disapprovingly. "What odd people they are!"

"People . . .?" Tony laughed to himself.

"And did you tell Anna that Greg must come and

44

fetch the plastic tree without fail?" Mum asked.

"No. She was in a hurry."

"So what are *we* supposed to do with the tree now?" asked his mother unhappily.

Tony shrugged. "No idea."

"I really don't like you having that tree in your room when the whole town's being searched for it!" she declared.

Tony grinned. "I could throw it out of the window, then the police will think Mrs Starling pinched it!"

"What a brilliant idea!" said his mother sarcastically. "The only trouble is, Mrs Starling would know immediately which flat the tree came from!"

"You two shouldn't get so worked up about all this," Dad put in. 'I bet you the newspaper people have got other far more exciting stories. A few plastic Christmas trees taken from the roof of a department store is hardly earth-shattering news!"

"I just hope you're right!" sighed Mum.

It seemed that Tony's father was right. The next day, Tony could find nothing more about it in the papers.

His mother behaved as though a weight had been lifted from her mind. "How do you feel about coming into town with me this afternoon and buying presents for Anna and Rudolph?" she suggested at lunch.

"Mm – yes," Tony said.

"You don't seem very excited at the idea."

"Well, I don't know what they'd like . . ."

"That really isn't a problem, when you see the choice there is nowadays!"

"Choice?" said Tony sceptically.

He was right: when they got to the book section of the department store his eyes swam – there were so many

45

different books on display. But he soon found out that there were hardly any titles to interest the Little Vampire.

"*Riding Holidays with John and Jane,*" exclaimed Tony's mother, holding out a thick volume. "Wouldn't that suit Rudolph?"

"No," growled Tony.

"Or this one: *The Yellow Seven's Secret Discovery?*"

"Rudolph doesn't like anything yellow."

"What about this, then? It's even won a prize . . ." She held out a picture book.

"Not that, please!" groaned Tony. "Rudolph would rip one of those into a thousand pieces!"

"What – do you mean he tears up books?" asked Mum, sounding startled.

Tony nodded. "He does if they're boring . . ."

"I see. We're obviously in the wrong place!" said Tony's mother sharply.

"No, wait!" exclaimed Tony. He had just found a book for Anna – *The Best Vampire Love Stories.*

"Vampire stories!" said Mum crossly. "Has Anna caught it off you?"

Tony stifled a smile. "Caught what?"

"Your craze on vampires!"

"Oh—" said Tony happily. "Anna didn't need to catch that!" He marched determinedly up to the till. *He* would buy this book for Anna, out of his own pocket money.

After a moment, his mother came up behind him. 'Here, if it can only be a vampire story," she said, holding out a thick book, "is this the sort of thing Rudolph would like?"

"*Vampires: Sixteen Black Tales for Those Who Love The Dark,*" Tony read. "That's a brilliant find, Mum!"

His mother smiled, looking rather pained. "If you think so, Tony . . ."

They paid for the books and then took the escalator to the toy department on the first floor.

Advisor on Presents

"What do *you* think? What would Anna and Rudolph like best?" asked Tony's mother, gesturing around them.

"Hmmm . . ." Tony didn't feel particularly happy with his rôle as advisor on presents. "What about a game . . .?"

"I was thinking of a cuddly toy," declared his mother, guiding the way to a shelf of furry animals. "What about this sweet little dog? Or this kitten?"

"Neither," said Tony. "It would have to be a wolf or a bat."

"Or a vampire, I know!" returned his mother heatedly. "But there's *nothing* like that here, as you can see!"

"Not yet . . ." said Tony.

His mother had moved over to the games.

"I can't tell much from the names," she said. " 'The Great Soap-Box Rally', 'Daddy Bear and His Friends', 'Let's Throw For A Gamble', 'Journey to the South Pole'—"

"Rudolph and Anna are only interested in exciting games," Tony told her.

"Well, I always think the old board games are the best." His mother pulled a large pale blue box down from the shelf. "Here: Draughts, Snakes and Ladders, Chess and Ludo."

Tony shook his head. "They've already got Ludo –

only they call it something different."

"Oh? What's that?"

"Blood-o!"

Sighing deeply, Tony's mother replaced the collection of games on the shelf. "What shall we do, then?" she asked.

"Perhaps we'd better split up." Tony thought he would be bound to have better ideas for presents without his mother's continual questions!

"All right," she said. "We'll meet up again in an hour by the CDs."

"I'm going to go back to the book department first," announced Tony. "I can't believe that there aren't a few more reasonable vampire stories among so many books!"

But Tony could only find ghost stories, and he was sure that Rudolph and Anna wouldn't be particularly interested in *The Water Spirit of Rockwool Castle* or *The Ghost With His Head Under His Arm*.

However, the illustrations in the books gave Tony a brilliant idea. He went off to the Household Goods department and chose some candles, red for Anna and black for Rudolph. He also bought a large family pack of matches, a red lighter and a black torch, as a joint present for both of them.

When he showed his purchases to his mother, she looked a little startled.

"Those are rather peculiar presents, aren't they?" she said.

"Peculiar?" repeated Tony indignantly.

"Candles, a lighter, a torch . . . That's squirrel behaviour."

"Squirrel behaviour?" Tony couldn't think what she was talking about.

"Yes. That's what it used to be called when people

started to hoard things for possible emergencies."

"It's not silly to lay down stores," said Tony.

"Why did you get ordinary household candles?" she asked contemptuously.

"They're supposed to last the longest," Tony told her.

She tried to laugh. "Well, I think the presents I've chosen are a bit more Christmassy!"

With that, she proudly produced *her* purchases. Tony paled. He suddenly realized that his suggestion that they split up to shop had been a gigantic mistake. He could agree to the make-up bag for Anna, complete with lipstick and powder, but the little stand-up mirror that went with them was a disaster!

For Rudolph, Mum had chosen a camera. A camera of all things, when vampires didn't have a reflection and their picture never came out in photographs!

"It was on special offer," she said, noticing Tony's look of disbelief.

"I —" He looked for the right words, "I don't think Rudolph will be very pleased with a camera."

"Why not?"

"He . . . he doesn't know how to take photographs." At least that was half true.

"Well, he'll have to learn then," Mum laughed. "Photography's a very nice hobby!"

"Rudolph doesn't have time for hobbies," retorted Tony. "And what's more, he hates learning!"

His mother sighed. "Well, if you're sure he won't use a camera, we'll have to go back straight away and exchange it."

"Can you do that?" exclaimed Tony.

"Yes, of course. After all, I want to give Rudolph something he'll like."

"Then you ought to exchange the mirror at the same

time," said Tony quickly.

"Why?"

"Well, because—" Tony cleared his throat, "they don't like mirrors at Anna's house."

"Really?" Tony's mother sounded very surprised. "Are they against mirrors for ideological reasons?"

"That's right!" said Tony. "Ideological reasons!"

His mother smiled. "Now you can see how little I know about your friends. It would be better if you came to advise me. Come along, Tony."

Tony followed her readily.

They exchanged the camera for a Walkman and six batteries. Tony bought two cassettes with his own money. Instead of the mirror, they chose a smart-looking book for Anna, with PRIVATE – Do Not Open in gold letters on it. It had a lock and a tiny silver key and it was a diary: you could write down everything that happened to you each day – or, in Anna's case, each night!

Vampires Have To Fend For Themselves

Tony got back home tired but happy. For the first time, he could understand why his mother always complained that the days leading up to Christmas were the most exhausting of the whole year.

Almost immediately after supper, he said goodnight to his parents and trotted off to his room. But he had hardly closed the door behind him before he was once again wide awake: outside, in front of the window, he could make out the outline of a large, dark figure. It could only be a vampire, a fully grown vampire . . .

And the vampire could certainly see *him*, because as soon as he came into the room, Tony had switched on the light. In fact, the vampire was already knocking impatiently on the glass.

Anxiously, Tony went over to the window.

"Hurry up! Move your lazy bones!" he heard Greg saying in his croaky voice. "There's a nasty sharp wind out here!"

"Coming—" With trembling fingers, Tony twisted the catch.

Greg jumped down into the room, once more accompanied by the smell of antiseptic mixed with the usual "perfume" of decay, planted himself directly in front of Tony, and said brightly, "Hallo, Tony!"

"Hallo!" Tony murmured, and then asked cautiously,

53

"Did you want to see my flat now?"

"Your flat?" Greg gave his grating laugh. "Where on earth did you dig that idea up? From a coffin?"

"You told me yourself you had to get used to a home full of Christmas decorations!"

"Oh, that—" Greg waved his hand dismissively. "Done that already!"

"Done it?" Tony was astonished.

"That's foxed you, hasn't it? But now *our* home's got its own Christmas decorations," Greg explained proudly. Then he added, looking pointedly at Tony's neck, "Vampires have to fend for themselves – that's an old family saying."

Tony felt himself going alternately hot and cold under Greg's gaze. He took a step towards his desk. He had put his hockey stick over there, just in case.

"If you haven't come because of Christmas, what do you want?" he asked uneasily.

Greg clicked his sharp teeth together. "What do I want?" he chuckled. Then he went on, almost tenderly, "Well, there *is* something I need from you . . ."

"Is there?" Tony groped for the hockey stick.

"Yes! Something that won't cost you a penny!" Greg laughed, running his tongue slowly over his lips.

Tony's throat felt as though something tight were tied round it. "I – I don't know what you mean," he stammered.

"Don't you?" said Greg. "I was relying on getting it from you . . ."

"Then – then it's just your bad luck!" retorted Tony, as bravely and firmly as he could.

"Surely you can spare me a little?" Greg's eyes seemed to bore through him.

"No!" Tony cried out. "No!" At last he had hold of

the hockey stick. He clutched it in his right hand. If Greg came a centimetre closer . . .

"Why, what's my friend Tony got there?" Without warning, Greg surged forward and pulled Tony's right arm into view. "A club?" He pretended to be surprised. "What do you want this great big club for, Tony?"

"For a start, it's not a club, it's my hockey stick," said Tony in a strangled voice. "And secondly, I'm going to defend myself with it if you—"

"If I what?"

"If you try . . . to bite me!"

"*Bite* you? Where on earth did you get that idea?"

"You said you wanted to get something from me – something that wouldn't cost me a penny!" cried Tony.

"Tony! Do you only ever think of one thing . . .?" Greg gave a menacing laugh. "I was talking about your advice – a piece of friendly advice!"

"My advice?" repeated Tony distrustfully.

"Yes!" Greg sat down on Tony's bed. "I need a couple of good tips from you – for Christmas presents!"

Tony gave a low groan. "No, not again!"

"What do you mean, again?" Greg roared. "This is the first time I've asked you for advice just because you're a friend!" The last words were uttered in such a menacing voice that Tony's skin began to prickle with goosepimples. "But if you don't want to be my friend, Tony Peasbody, I can change my mind too!" He got up and walked towards Tony.

"I – I didn't mean it like that," Tony said hastily. "Of course I'd like to be your friend."

"Then out with some tips!"

"First I need to know who the presents are for."

"Who for? Well, one for Sniveller and one for McRookery, dimwit!"

Tony put the hockey stick back in its place to gain time. "How about some strong after-shave for Sniveller – one you can all smell a mile off, before he gets anywhere near you?"

"Brilliant!" said Greg approvingly, digging Tony in the ribs with his finger – the one with the nail filed to a point. "You amaze me! But that's only *one* present!" he rumbled in his usual demanding way, after a pause. "Come on, get thinking! I need two presents!"

You Can Always Make Things Happen

Tony's mind raced. "Do you know whether McRookery smokes?" he said.

"I'm sure he doesn't!" replied Greg.

"You can always make things happen! You ought to give him a pipe and some tobacco. Then he'll smoke at night in the cemetery and you'll have a warning if he's coming."

Greg twisted his lips into a grin. "You're not as stupid as I thought. But where am I going to get a pipe and tobacco from?" Suddenly his face lit up. "I know, *you* can buy them for me!" he said. "You're my friend!"

"What if I haven't got any money left?" retorted Tony.

"No money?" Greg chuckled. "Then you'll have to get hold of some from somewhere! Money's there for the taking!"

"I see – the same way as you got hold of the Christmas trees," said Tony grimly. "You realize, don't you, that the police are on the trail of whoever did it."

For a moment, Greg was speechless. "The police?"

"Yes, they are! And there's a long article about it in the paper. With a photo."

"A photo?" Now Greg was completely confused. "A photo of me? That can't be true! We vampires can't have our photos taken . . ."

"Not of you! Of the roof of the department store!"

Tony corrected him.

"Oh, I see." Greg gave a sigh of relief. "Huh! What's so special about the roof of the store that anyone should want to take a photo of it?" he said mockingly, probably to cover up his embarrassment.

"Exactly! That's just it!" said Tony. "It's a photo of an empty roof, because you were crazy enough to steal all the Christmas trees!"

"I wouldn't call it crazy," Greg told him, chuckling proudly. "I'd call it daring – daring and heroic!"

"Heroic? Well, you'll be able to put your heroism to the test soon," remarked Tony.

'What – what are you talking about?" Greg was puzzled.

"Simple – when they come and search your vault!" Greg opened his eyes wide.

"Our vault? Who's going to come and search the vault?"

"Just think. They'll soon find out it wasn't a cat-burglar or someone with a helicopter, as they suggested in the newspaper article. Then they'll assume it was vampires. And where will they come and look? In the cemetery, of course!"

"Tony!" Greg's voice suddenly sounded very small. "You're frightening me. Police in our cemetery . . . By Dracula, we'll have to emigrate!"

"It's not as bad as all that!" Tony comforted him. "There's nothing about it in the paper today, and Dad said the reporters have got lots of other stories which are more important."

"Perhaps the reporters have, but what about the police?" Greg retorted.

"Well, if I were you, I'd put the Christmas trees back," declared Tony.

"Put them back? What's the use of that?"

"It'll help you, of course! If the trees are back on the

roof, the police won't have any reason to investigate the crime any more!"

"Yes, you're right!" Greg clapped his hand to his forehead, as though he'd thought of the solution himself. "Don't despair, Greg'll take care!" he announced boastfully, adding, "I'd better get my skates on! I'm afraid I'll have to take this lovely thing with me too," he said, pointing to Tony's plastic tree.

"Really? What a shame!" Tony found it hard to keep a straight face.

Greg picked up the plastic tree and clutched it firmly under one arm. "Don't forget to sort out the Christmas presents, whatever you do!" he told Tony, adding in a burst of croaky laughter, "Tony, my friend!"

Then he flew off into the night sky.

Over the Cemetery Walls and Beyond

Tony watched him go, feeling doubly relieved. Greg was the sort of "friend" it was best to see the back of! And without the revolting tree, his room was nice and cosy once more.

Suddenly, he went hot and cold all over. Even if he wouldn't miss the monstrous object, his mother was bound to ask where he had put the plastic tree.

He quickly sat down at his desk and wrote a notice. "Entry strictly forbidden. Christmas present construction taking place in this room!"

Underlining the words "Christmas present construction" three times in red, he fixed the notice to the outside of his door, crept into bed and opened the first of the *Sixteen Black Tales*. If he was going to read all sixteen before Christmas, he would have to get a move on!

Later he heard his parents crossing the hall. They stopped outside Tony's door and whispered to each other about the notice. Just as he had expected, they didn't open the door, just asked softly whether he was asleep yet. When Tony made no answer, they crept away again.

The next morning, Tony asked his mother for a "Christmas bonus" on top of his pocket money. "I still need to buy felt-tips and coloured paper," he explained.

Obviously delighted, Mum gave him an extra five pounds.

Tony thought for a moment. If he put his other five pounds with it, it might just stretch to cover McRookery and Sniveller's presents.

After school, he went straight to the toiletries department of the department store. He had hoped he would be able to try out all the different brands of after-shave undisturbed, until he found the strongest-smelling one. However, after only a short time, a large, heavily made-up sales lady appeared and asked brusquely, "May I help you?"

"What do you mean?" asked Tony. "Isn't it self-service here?"

"Not for little boys who don't want to buy anything," she answered shortly.

Tony drew himself up. "For a start, I'm not little. And for another thing, I'm looking for after-shave."

"After-shave? Why don't you come back in four years' time?" she said.

"Four years?" Tony grinned. "Does that mean you haven't got a very wide range at the moment?"

"What do you mean?" she asked, sounding irritated.

"Well, you told me to come back in four years' time!"

The sales lady flushed pink under the thick layer of make-up and powder. "What a cheek!" she hissed, turning away.

"Actually, I've already made up my mind," said Tony, taking down a medium-sized bottle from the shelf, labelled "Autumn Spice". The smell had been by far the strongest.

"But that's for older men," remarked the sales lady spitefully.

"Exactly!" said Tony with a grin.

In the tobacco department, he was lucky and no one disturbed him. The two young girls at the till were deep in conversation and didn't take the slightest notice of him. So Tony was left in peace and chose a cheap but – in his opinion – expensive-looking pipe and some tobacco that smelled like vanilla. The pong would certainly spread right over the cemetery walls and beyond!

That evening, Tony waited impatiently for Greg, but he didn't come. His parents didn't put in an appearance either: as "modern" parents, they respected the notice forbidding entry posted on his door. So they didn't yet know that the plastic tree had gone from his bedroom.

The next morning, as Tony's mother was reading the *News and Mail*, she suddenly exclaimed, "Hey! The Christmas trees are back again!"

Tony felt his tummy turn over. "Really?" he said, holding out his hand in the hope that she would give him the newspaper. But instead, she began to read aloud.

" '14th December. **Christmas Tree Robbery now even more mysterious!** The stolen trees are back again once more on the roof of the department store! Harry Clamp (43), manager of the store, discovered the artificial trees yesterday evening as he did his rounds with his dog.

"Yet again, the circumstances surrounding the incident are completely mystifying. The iron door had not been broken through, nor was there any sign of a ladder or any other means of climbing up to the roof. Since there is still no clue as to the motive of the perpetrators, we can only hope that such an event will not reoccur."

Tony's mother looked up from the newspaper. "Why didn't you tell me about this?"

"What was there to tell?" asked Tony cautiously.

"That Greg had come to his senses."

"His *senses?*" Tony nearly choked, he found this such a funny expression to use in connection with . . . a vampire!

"Of course," said his mother. "It not just that Greg realized what a foolish mistake he made – he's even put the trees back! That's the hardest thing of all: not simply to have the insight to know when you've done something wrong, but to put it right again!"

Tony bit his lip and kept silent. In Greg's case, "insight" was hardly the right word – "far-sight" was more like it, for fear of police investigations!

"When did you give the tree back to him?" his mother wanted to know.

Tony gave a start. "When? Yesterday," he said. "When you went for a walk round the block." Just in time, he remembered the half-hour stroll his parents had taken in the evening.

"Did Greg call at the front door at exactly that time?" she asked in disbelief.

"No," Tony grinned. "He knocked on the window and I gave him the tree!"

"Yeah, yeah!" said his mother, sounding annoyed. "If you believe that, you'll believe anything!"

Tony shook his head. "If you believe that, you'll turn into a vampire!" He got up, feeling pleased. "Now I must go and do some homework."

He stopped in front of his bedroom door. He didn't actually need the notice any more, but after thinking for a moment, he decided to leave it up. After all, he might have a visitor that evening!

Moth=Off

However, Tony was disappointed. No one came on Friday evening either.

At last it was Saturday, the evening the Little Vampire had promised to come. This time, Tony's parents had decided to go to the cinema.

"Are you going to see a vampire film?" Tony asked cheekily as he said goodbye. His father laughed. "You could call it that."

"Really?" Tony was surprised.

"Of course not!" his mother put him right. "We're going to a political film."

"That isn't necessarily a contradiction," joked Dad. "Some of our politicians are quite vampirish!"

"I agree!" said Tony. "Some of them are even worse than real vampires!"

"Since when have you been interested in politics?" Mum asked pointedly.

Tony grinned. "Ever since we had a discussion in school about vampires – er, I mean, politics!"

Once Tony was alone, he pulled the curtains back and switched on the TV. "What's the betting that . . ." yet again, there wasn't a vampire film on that evening? As he was running through the various channels, something knocked on the window. "Rudolph!" he exclaimed, running over.

It was: there outside sat the Little Vampire. He slipped

down into the room and pointed to the TV, where a children's choir was trilling "Tie a yellow ribbon round the old oak tree . . ."

"Yuk! Yellow!" spat the Little Vampire. "So that's the sort of thing they waste broadcasts on!"

"It's typical Saturday evening stuff," Tony told him. He wished he could hold his nose. The "scent" of cleaning chemicals wafted round Rudolph. It was almost more penetrating than Greg's aroma.

"But we're not going to waste *our* time with such nonsense!" the Little Vampire was saying. "Come on Tony, let's fly!"

"How?" retorted Tony. "I haven't got a cloak!"

Chuckling, the Little Vampire pulled a second cloak out from under his own and held it out to Tony. "Here, you can keep this one for the moment."

"Is it Uncle Theodore's?" asked Tony.

"Yes," the vampire told him. "It's been soaking in Moth-Off for three days."

"Moth-Off?" murmured Tony. His jeans and jumper were bound to pick up the revolting stink!

"Anna concocted the mixture, actually," the Little Vampire revealed.

"Anna?"

"Yes. I don't know exactly what went into it, but there were certainly flowers from the stink-bomb tree, and lots of camphor too, of course."

Tony shuddered. "It's not a very nice smell."

"It's not supposed to smell nice!" retorted the Little Vampire. "The name means, 'Moths, push off'! If they don't want to push off of their own accord, then something's got to be done to help them. What is it?" he hissed. Tony had still not put on the cloak. "Are you ill or something?"

"No . . ." Hesitantly, Tony pulled the cloak around him. If he didn't want all his friends to "push off " on Monday, he would have to put his clothes through the wash tomorrow morning!

"Where are we flying?" he asked.

"Where?" The Little Vampire jumped up on to the window-sill. "The whole night is ours!" he cried, flying out of the window.

Tony looked down uneasily. He hoped he wasn't going to faint from all the fumes streaming out of the black material! He spread out his arms and moved them up and down a couple of times. With a beating heart, he felt his feet rise off the floor. So the cloak was still fit for flying!

Tony moved his arms more strongly and followed the Little Vampire. It was a relatively mild December night, but cold enough to make his breath stream away like a white flag.

"Wait for me!" he called after the Little Vampire. "I've got to go back for something."

"Go back? Why?"

"I want to put something else on – gloves and a thicker jumper."

"You really are a wimp!" remarked the Little Vampire.

"I am not!" retorted Tony.

"Look at me!" The Little Vampire raised his cloak with one hand. Tony could see black woolly tights and a short brown tunic with a belt.

"*We* wear the same things in summer and winter," boasted the vampire.

"Yeah, sure," said Tony. "But I bet you've got at least five extra pairs of tights underneath!"

The Little Vampire gave an embarrassed laugh. "Three, actually," he murmured softly. Then he snorted, "And I suppose you're wearing some of your revolting long white thermal underwear!"

"No, but I will be any minute now!" Tony told him. "I don't usually wear them at home in the flat!"

"OK, then," said the Little Vampire. "I'll wait for you at the playground."

Ten minutes later, Tony was back wearing his thick Norwegian wool pullover, padded skiing trousers and woolly gloves.

"What a pity you rushed off like that," the Little Vampire greeted him.

"Pity?"

"Yes. You'd just gone when I remembered an old family remedy. If you use it, you'll never be cold again, believe me!"

"A family remedy?" repeated Tony, full of misgiving.

The Little Vampire giggled behind his hand. "You have to get your *blood* circulating – that's the secret!"

Tony pretended he hadn't understood what the Little Vampire was getting at.

"That's what our sports teacher says too," he agreed. "Every lesson he says, 'Get moving, kids! That'll get your circulation going!' "

The Little Vampire grinned. " 'Moving' isn't part of our remedy at all – it's more important that you . . . keep still!"

"Keep still?" Tony said indignantly. "That would do quite the opposite in these temperatures! Or do you want me to turn into an icicle hanging around in this cold?"

"No!" spat the Little Vampire. "You really can't take a joke, can you?"

"I can," said Tony, "but jokes stop when it comes to my blood circulation!"

"Egoist!" growled the Little Vampire, moving his arms so violently that he shot straight up into the air. Tony had to set to work with a will in order to catch up with him again.

Christmas Frenzy

"You still haven't told me where we're going," Tony reminded the Little Vampire when he caught up with him. Below, he could already make out the line of the cemetery wall.

"Huh! Perhaps I don't feel like doing anything with you any more," answered the Little Vampire.

"Why not?"

"Why not? *Why not?* Because you've spoilt the whole Christmas mood for me, that's why!"

"Christmas mood?" Tony was amazed. "Already?"

"Yes, already," the Little Vampire told him, adding mysteriously, "They start early at McRookery's!"

"Do they?"

"That's it." The Little Vampire chuckled. "Wait till you see his house: it's like Father Christmas's own home!"

"Are we flying to McRookery's, then?" asked Tony uneasily.

"Yes!" The Little Vampire flew in an elegant sweep over the white cemetery wall, then floated gently down to earth on the far side of McRookery's garden.

Tony landed next to him, full of foreboding.

"I just don't know what's up with McRookery!" the Little Vampire pointed to the lighted living room window. "Last year he didn't make any fuss at all about Christmas. This time, he's got a Christmas tree as tall

and wide as a –" he searched for the right description " – as tall and wide as a coffin!"

Even Tony could see the Christmas tree. A tall blond man was decorating it: it was Sniveller!

"Where's McRookery?" asked Tony in a whisper.

"I expect he's busy baking Christmas biscuits!" joked the vampire.

"I don't think that's very funny!" said Tony.

"That's because you're a spoilsport!" replied the Little Vampire.

"Or because *I'm* the only one who's keeping a clear head in all this," retorted Tony grimly. "You all seem to be caught up in this Christmas frenzy!"

The vampire giggled again. "That's right! Aunt Dorothy was really disappointed when Greg had to take those pretty Christmas trees back again."

"Was she?"

"Yes. She said the trees reminded her of our home in Transylvania. Do you know what 'Transylvania' means?"

"No idea."

"It means 'behind the woods'. Anyhow, Greg's going to get hold of some new Christmas trees for us," he announced.

"Oh, no!" groaned Tony.

"You seem to begrudge us everything!" hissed the Little Vampire.

"I certainly don't like you having stolen Christmas trees!" Tony told him.

The vampire snorted contemptuously. "Well? What else can we do? For a start, we haven't got any money, and secondly, the shops have been shut for ages by the time we're out and about. Or would you like to buy us ten Christmas trees out of your pocket money?" he asked abruptly.

"Perhaps, if I had enough," said Tony. "My last few pounds have gone on presents for Sniveller and McRookery."

"What?" The Little Vampire stared at Tony in total amazement. "Have you been invited to McRookery's Christmas party too?"

"No. But I had to buy the presents for Greg."

"That was clever of him," Rudolph nodded appreciatively. "How did Greg manage to get round you when you're so tight-fisted?"

"Tight-fisted?" Tony repeated, sounding hurt. "*You* certainly haven't got any reason to call me stingy!"

"Haven't I?" the Little Vampire grinned. "What if I said 'tight-necked' instead of tight-fisted? You've never been very generous in that respect . . . But enough of that," he said. "Tell me how Greg got round you."

At the words "tight-*necked*", Tony had taken a step back. "How did he get round me?" he said. "He made out that we were friends."

"Huh! Greg's got friends all over the place," remarked the Little Vampire in amusement, pointing to the lighted window.

McRookery had just come into the living room. He said something to Sniveller and then both went out of the room.

"Come on, let's take a closer look at the Christmas tree," whispered the Little Vampire.

Vampires! Vampires!

They ran across the patio on tiptoe. Unfortunately, McRookery's was one of those "well cared for" gardens where the lawn looks as though it's been trimmed with nail scissors. There were no hedges or bushes to speak of, and the only camouflage on the patio was a large flower tub, which had been decorated with pine branches.

Tony and the Little Vampire ducked down behind the tub and peered into the room. The first thing Tony noticed wasn't the Christmas tree – there was nothing particularly unusual about that – it was the collection of unusual pieces of wood hanging on the wall. Old and new, some beautifully carved, some quite simple – they were all wooden stakes!

Stakes like those meant only one thing: the complete destruction of the vampires . . .

"Rudolph!" he stammered, digging the vampire in the ribs. But Rudolph was gazing as if enchanted at the decorated tree.

"Those little figures over there –" The Little Vampire gave a deep sigh " – the ones with the long silver hair . . . they're just like my Olga!"

"You'd do better to look at what's hanging on the wall," Tony said severely.

"Huh! You can worry about the wall!" hissed the Little Vampire. Then he went on, in a dreamy voice, "I don't suppose McRookery would let me have one of those sweet little figures, would he?"

"He's more likely to give you one of his wooden stakes!" retorted Tony.

The Little Vampire cried out in anger. "Why do you always have to spoil things for me?" he exclaimed. "Can't I just forget for five minutes that I'm a vampire?"

"That could be very dangerous," Tony said. "Especially since there are at least thirty wooden stakes hanging on the wall over there!"

"Oh Dracula, no . . .!" At last the Little Vampire seemed to have seen the stakes. Slowly he stood up and took a step towards the window.

"What are you going to do?" cried Tony. Just then the door to the living room opened and Sniveller came in, carrying a fully laden tray.

Just in time, Tony managed to grab hold of Rudolph's cloak and drag him back behind the flower tub. Meanwhile, Sniveller had carried the tray to a table by the window, where he set out two cups, a teapot and a plate of open sandwiches with various toppings. When he had finished, he poured some sort of red liquid into the cups.

"That red stuff . . . what is it?" asked the Little Vampire huskily.

"Henry, are you coming?" called Sniveller. "I've just poured out!"

"I expect it's only tea," whispered Tony. "Rose-hip tea, probably!"

"Yuk! Tea!" spat the Little Vampire. "Never again!"

At this point, McRookery appeared. He looked briefly over at the window, but since the room was so well lit, he didn't see the two spies out on the patio.

Tony held his breath. Suddenly, to his horror, he felt his nose start to tickle. He couldn't help it – he had to sneeze! The noise seemed as loud as a drum-roll to him, but – Dracula be thanked! – it didn't seem to have reached the two nightwatchmen sitting inside at the table.

"Have you gone mad?" spat the Little Vampire.

"No, I've just caught a cold," said Tony, sounding subdued. "Have you got a handkerchief?"

"Yes, here!" said the vampire darkly, holding out a piece of cloth to Tony. It didn't look particularly clean, but that didn't matter because he could feel that awful tickling in his nose again.

"I—" he began, sneezing for the second time. This time, both McRookery and Sniveller heard it. Their heads turned.

"Vampires!" yelled McRookery, jumping up from the table. China fell to the floor with a crash, Sniveller shrieked, "Oh no, the carpet!" and then the garden door was flung open.

By then, Tony and the Little Vampire were already several metres up in the air, safe from McRookery who was running up and down the patio as if he'd been stung by a hornet, and roaring, "Vampires! Vampires!"

"Huh! If you didn't have me . . ." said the Little Vampire.

"I – I don't know what happened," Tony murmured.

"You and your stupid sneezes! You'd have stayed down there frozen like a pillar of salt, or rather, a pillar of sneezing powder!" said the Little Vampire grimly. "If I hadn't grabbed you by the cloak and pulled you up with me, you'd be in McRookery's clutches by now!"

"I just didn't realize . . ."

"Obviously! Now, come on!"

"Where are we going?" Once more Tony felt his nose tickle, but this time he managed to stifle the sneeze.

"You'll find out soon enough," replied the Little Vampire brusquely. Below them stood the church tower. Beyond it, Tony could make out the first houses of the estate where he lived.

"Aren't we going to do something else?" he asked. "You said yourself, the night belonged to us."

"And bed belongs to people who are ill!" retorted the vampire curtly.

"But I'm not ill! I've only got a bit of a cold!" Tony contradicted him.

But the Little Vampire's mind was made up. When they reached Tony's block, he wished him a "Get well soon!" and prepared to fly away again.

"Stop!" cried Tony. "You never told me whether you're going to come over at Christmas."

"Of course I'm coming!" replied the vampire. "Do you think I want to be the only one to come away from Christmas empty-handed?" Cackling with laughter, he fluttered away.

Transylvanian 'Flu

The next morning Tony realized he'd caught more than just a cold: his head burned, and he had a dull pain behind his forehead.

It hurt to swallow, too. He could only eat half of one of the delicious rolls his father had baked, and he didn't touch his hot chocolate at all.

"Are you ill, Tony?" His mother sounded worried.

"Hmm, don't know," he answered. He suddenly began to shiver in spite of his warm dressing-gown.

"Have you got a temperature?" she asked.

"Maybe . . ." By now, Tony was feeling so weak and dizzy that he hardly protested as his father took him back to bed and his mother appeared with a thermometer. He didn't even mind that she stayed sitting on his bed while she took his temperature.

"39 degrees!" she exclaimed, as she read the thermometer. "And it's only first thing in the morning! We'll have to call Doctor Dozee!"

An hour later, Doctor Dozee, their family doctor, appeared and diagnosed 'flu. Tony would have to stay in bed for a couple of days, be a good boy and drink the medicine she prescribed, and rest.

"I'm sure you'll be better by Christmas Eve," she promised.

"Hope so," said Tony feebly.

"Course you will!" She smiled cheerfully. "The

thought of all those Christmas presents will help you get back on your feet in no time."

She wasn't far off the mark. Tony still hadn't finished the presents for his parents, and he just couldn't afford to lie in bed for long!

But first, he did want to have a good, long sleep. So when his mother asked how it was possible that he could have caught such a serious bout of 'flu overnight, he snapped at her, "Didn't you hear? I've got to rest!" and turned to face the wall.

Tony stayed in bed all Monday. By Tuesday, his temperature had gone and by Wednesday, Doctor Dozee said he could get up for a couple of hours. It was 20th December.

Tony started to worry about the Christmas party with Anna and Rudolph. In the past few evenings, neither had come knocking on his window. Nor had Greg appeared to collect his presents.

Supposing Doctor Dozee's medicine had made Tony fall into such a deep sleep that he had never heard their knock? No, someone like Greg would have hammered on the glass till the window was opened! Nor were Anna and Rudolph exactly shy when it came to waking Tony. Perhaps the vampires were so busy with their own preparations for Christmas that they didn't have time to worry about anything else. After all, when they were on McRookery's patio, Tony himself had remarked that the vampires all seemed to have been caught up in the "Christmas frenzy"! One thing was certain: if he hadn't caught this horrible 'flu, he would have flown off to the cemetery and tried to meet up with Anna and Rudolph. But as things stood, there was nothing he could do except wait.

When there was a knock on his window on Thursday, shortly after nine o'clock, Tony was really relieved.

He pulled open the window and found himself looking into the pale face of the Little Vampire.

"At last!" he said.

The Little Vampire grinned. "We don't always get such a friendly greeting," he said, slipping down into the room.

"You're right there!" said Tony.

"Always am," replied the Little Vampire, sounding pleased with himself.

"No, not always," Tony contradicted him. "But this time you were right when you said 'Ill people belong in bed.' I've been quite poorly up till now."

"You do look a little pale," remarked the Little Vampire. "But", he corrected Tony, "I didn't say 'Ill people belong in bed', I said, 'Bed belongs to people who are ill!' "

Tony groaned weakly. "But that's the same thing!"

"Not at all!" retorted the Little Vampire. "It's those tiny differences that matter."

"Do they?" said Tony scornfully.

"Yes!" hissed the vampire. "But you've obviously got a memory like a hairnet, only with even more holes!" He came nearer and studied the woollen scarf that Tony had wound around his neck. "Is it possible that you've . . . been eating the wrong sort of food?" he cackled.

"You'd better stay right where you are!" Tony warned him. "If you catch what I've got, you won't be able to come to our Christmas party!"

"What do you mean, catch?" The Little Vampire hesitated. "Since when has a strained neck been catching?"

"I haven't strained my neck!" Tony told him. "I've got an inflamed throat!"

"Inflamed?" said Rudolph, puzzled. "Do you mean you've got a temperature and a sore throat? Yuck!"

"That's right," Tony told him, and just to pay him back for the remark about the hairnet, he added boastfully, "I've got Transylvanian 'flu!"

It would have been better not to have said that. The Little Vampire gave a shout of anger and shrank back to the window. "You've got Transylvanian 'flu?" he cried.

"Yes, so what?" said Tony, surprised at the Little Vampire's violent reaction.

"That's the most terrible 'flu there is!" groaned the Little Vampire. "Do you know what the worst thing about it is?" By now, he had jumped on to the window-sill and was holding a corner of his cloak protectively in front of his nose and mouth.

"No," said Tony, puzzled.

"It's the only illness in the world against which we have nothing to defend ourselves!" exclaimed the Little Vampire.

"But—" Tony began, but the vampire had already flown away. He ran to the window. "I was wrong!" he called. "It isn't Transylvanian 'flu! it's Trans-Siberian 'flu!"

Christmas Kisses

Tony stood shivering by the window, gazing out into the night. He felt utterly miserable: not because he wasn't well, but because he regretted the tasteless "joke" which had thrown Rudolph into such a panic.

"Are you ill?" came a bright voice suddenly.

Silently, a small dark figure floated out of the sky and landed on the window-sill. It was Anna!

"If you are, you ought to close the window quickly!" she said.

"Mm, yes." Tony gave an embarrassed cough.

She hopped down into the room and Tony shut the window behind her.

"Does it make you feel horrid, this Siberian 'flu?" Anna asked, gazing at him with wide eyes.

Tony became aware of a lovely smell of roses coming from her cloak – the scent of "Fragrance of Eternal Love"!

"Well, it's like this," he began. "I've just got 'flu, but Rudolph said my memory was as full of holes as a hairnet – and of course I couldn't let him get away with that. So I told him I had Transylvanian 'flu."

"*Transylvanian* 'flu?" exclaimed Anna, obviously dismayed. "But you just called out of the window something about Siberian 'flu . . ."

"Yes, because I wanted Rudolph to come back!"

"You *would* have to say Transylvanian 'flu . . ."

Anna looked thoughtful. "Dozens of vampires have already fallen victim to it – Rudolph only escaped by a whisker!"

"What? Rudolph too?"

"For thirteen nights he hovered between life and death," Anna declared.

Tony cleared his throat. "I thought . . . he'd been dead for a long time."

Now Anna was smiling, looking embarrassed. "Even so, we can still fall ill," she said. "And it's far, far worse for us than for you humans. We have to lie in hard coffins, in damp, unheated tombs – and we can't even go to the doctor! What's more," she went on, "Transylvanian 'flu strikes at our very heart and soul!"

"Does it?"

"Yes! It makes us lose all our – er, energy. Some vampires get so depressed that they go and lie out in the sun!" Anna gulped.

"Is that so?" murmured Tony. If only he'd known that before!

"You . . . you absolutely must talk to Rudolph!" he pleaded. "You must tell him that it was only a stupid joke of mine and that I'm really, truly sorry!"

"I only hope he'll believe me," replied Anna. "How's your bout of 'flu going?"

"Oh, I'm much better now," Tony told her. "Luckily! Otherwise I'm sure my parents would have put off the Christmas party to another day."

"Put it off?"

"Yes – to Boxing Day or the day after. But now everything can stay just the way it was."

"And everything's just the way it was between us too!" Anna said, gazing at Tony. He felt himself going red.

"We must have a talk about how we're going to

manage it all," he said hastily, to change the subject.

"What do you mean, 'all'?" asked Anna, gazing deep into his eyes.

Tony looked away in embarrassment. "Well, you know, all the details to do with the Christmas party!"

"Oh, that!" Anna giggled. "You mean, whether I ought to sit on your right or your left, and whether you'll give me a Christmas kiss first, or I'll give you one!"

Tony didn't let his feelings show. "Christmas kisses?" he drawled. "I've never heard of them!"

"Haven't you?" Anna pouted. "What do people do then on Christmas Eve?"

"That's just what I want to talk to you about!" Tony declared. "You see, first the children have to wait outside, in the kitchen or in their rooms, while their parents decorate the Christmas tree and put the presents round it. As soon as they've finished, they ring the Christmas bells – at least, that's what we do at our house. After that, it's time to give out the presents."

"Do you always get what you want?" asked Anna. "My grandmother, Sabina the Sinister, has a funny expression: she always says, 'This is a fine kettle of fish!' when she doesn't get what she's expecting."

"Yes, I know what you mean!" Tony agreed. "Like when you get a voucher for a vacation venture," he added, remembering his present last Christmas!

Anna giggled. "What do you mean? It was such fun when we 'ventured' about together, you and me, in the Vale of Doom!"

"Yes, well, after the presents have been given out, it's time for the special Christmas dinner," Tony went on, unruffled.

"A shadow flitted across Anna's face. "What do you have for . . . your special Christmas dinner?"

85

"Goose à la Peasbody – same as every year."

"Hmm – I think perhaps Rudolph and I shouldn't arrive till after dinner!"

"You can't, that would be too late," Tony told her. "You absolutely must be there when the presents are given out, whatever happens, otherwise my parents will be disappointed."

"Only your parents?" asked Anna.

"Me too, of course!" Tony assured her hastily, adding, "especially because of the presents for you two!"

"For us?" Anna clenched her fists. "Why do I have to have stupid brothers!"

Tony started. "What do you mean? Is Greg coming too?"

"No. He's celebrating with McRookery and Sniveller," Anna said soothingly. After a pause, she asked, "What happens after you've eaten?"

"We play games."

"Games?" Anna's eyes lit up. "Like 'Squeak, Piggy, Squeak!' where we sit on each other's laps?"

"No, board games."

"Bored games?" Anna thought for a moment. "I don't want to be bored!"

"You won't be," Tony smiled. "They're games you play on a board – Coppit, Ludo, draughts and Snakes and Ladders."

Anna giggled. "If we can change Ludo into Blood-o, then I'd love to play!" She glanced across at the window. "I must fly now, Tony," she said. "Aunt Dorothy's waiting for me."

Tony gave a start. "Aunt Dorothy? You don't mean she's waiting outside my window?"

"No, in the vault. Greg's found some new Christmas trees. I'm supposed to be helping Aunt Dorothy put them up."

"New Christmas trees?" asked Tony suspiciously. "Do you know by any chance where he got them from?"

"No idea," she said evenly, "but they're much nicer than the others."

Oh, no! thought Tony. He just hoped Greg hadn't made off with the Christmas trees from the front of the town hall. As usual, they were the biggest, best and most expensive trees in town! There would be a gigantic fuss in the newspapers if that was what he'd done.

"Is there anything else we ought to discuss?" Anna was asking.

Tony thought for a moment. "No, I don't think so," he said.

"Then I'll see you the day after tomorrow," Anna said. "And be prepared!" she added mysteriously.

"For what?" asked Tony uneasily. That sounded so . . . menacing!

"For two unusual friends!" Anna burst out laughing. Then she quickly put a hand to her mouth, probably so that Tony wouldn't see her long vampire teeth!

"Goodnight!" she said softly. She went to the window, opened it and flew away.

Waiting for Vampire Claus

At lunch the next day, Tony opened the *News and Mail* with mixed feelings. But there wasn't any mention of Christmas trees going missing. He breathed a sigh of relief. Obviously Greg had learned his lesson from the department store tree affair!

"I'm amazed you're calm enough to read the newspaper," remarked his mother.

"What do you mean?" he asked.

"Well, it's only two days to Christmas and I think I'm more excited than you!" she smiled. "Still, it is rather unusual to be celebrating Christmas with two strangers."

"Two strangers?" exclaimed Tony indignantly. "Anna and Rudolph are my best friends!"

"Even so, we hardly know them," answered his mother. "And *you* haven't exactly helped Dad and me," she added reproachfully.

"How am I supposed to have helped you?"

"Well, when we asked you what Anna and Rudolph liked best to eat and drink, instead of giving us some clues, you just played the clown again!"

"Me? A clown?"

"Yes. In any case, I have *not* been to the chemist to get hold of some bottled blood, as you suggested." She sighed. "Now Rudolph and Anna will just have to be content with what your father and I have bought." She poured herself some coffee and went on, "But I do have one favour to ask you, Tony!"

"What's that?"

"Don't talk about vampires on Christmas Eve!"

Tony bit his lip. "That suits me fine!"

"You agree?" She looked at him in surprise.

"I certainly do!"

"So we really won't bring up the subject of vampires on Christmas Eve?" Tony's mother wanted to make quite sure.

"No," said Tony calmly. Why should they talk *about* vampires when they would be talking *to* vampires.

The rest of the day and the following day flashed by for Tony, who was kept busy putting finishing touches to his presents, tidying the flat and lending a hand in the kitchen.

At last it was 24th December! When Tony looked out of his window in the morning, instead of the snow he'd been hoping for, he saw rain running down the pane in thin streams.

"Poor drivers!" said his mother at breakfast.

"What do you mean?" asked Tony.

"They said on the radio that the roads are slippery as glass," Dad told him.

"Well, that won't affect us," said Tony.

"It will," Mum contradicted him. "After all, we're expecting guests. I'm sure Anna and Rudolph's parents will be bringing them over in the car, won't they?" She looked at Tony questioningly.

"Will they?" He could have replied that they would be flying, like all vampires, but remembering his promise, he simply said, "No, they'll be coming on foot."

"Well, I hope they don't slip over! I expect they'll have put grit down on the pavements, but even so . . ."

Tony's mother stopped.

"I promise you they won't slip over," Tony said.

But when it began to get dark and Anna and Rudolph still hadn't arrived, Mum began to get twitchy.

"Don't you think we should at least give their parents a ring?" she suggested.

"What good would that do?" Tony wanted to know.

"Well, at least we would know when Anna and Rudolph had set out."

"Perhaps they haven't set out yet," retorted Tony. "Perhaps they're still lying in—" "their coffins" was what he was about to say, but at the last minute he realized what he had almost let slip " —in a nice warm bath," he finished cunningly.

"Now?" His mother looked at him in astonishment. "Nobody spends Christmas Eve lounging around in the bath!"

Tony grinned. His mother was right in two ways: nobody, and certainly no vampire, would be lying in the bath!

"Why don't we watch television for a while?" suggested Dad. "Then the time won't drag so much."

"If we watch television, it'll go by even more slowly!" Tony contradicted him. "Have you seen what they've got on this Christmas?"

"What do you mean?" Dad picked up the paper that showed the television programmes. " 'Waiting for Santa Claus' – that sounds very nice!"

"Nice!" growled Tony.

"But of course, the people who arrange the programmes don't cater for your unusual tastes," his dad remarked.

"What do you mean, 'unusual'?" inquired Tony.

"Well, as far as you're concerned, the programme

probably ought to be called 'Waiting for Vampire Claus'!"

"You said it!"

"But there aren't any vampires on telly this Christmas!" Tony's father laughed.

"No, not on telly . . ." said Tony looking over at his mother with an innocent expression. After all, *he* hadn't brought the conversation round to vampires!

Happy Christmas!

Just after six o'clock, there was a ring at the door.

"At last!" said Tony's mum.

"I'll get it!" cried Tony, rushing out into the hall.

Anna and the Little Vampire were standing at the door. They didn't look exactly "Christmassy" – their faces were brightly coloured but strangely blotchy, and over their vampire cloaks they wore thin rubber waterproofs that gleamed with rain – the vampires' version of a raincoat. Even worse, they smelled terribly of decay and musty coffins.

"Good evening, Tony!" Anna said tenderly.

"Hallo, Anna!" he replied.

"Aren't you going to say hallo to me then!" hissed the Little Vampire. "Has your Siberian 'flu made you lose your voice?"

Tony felt himself going red. "Hallo, Rudolph," he said. "It's so nice that you could come," he added.

"What dreadful rain!" Anna complained. "Proper onion weather!"

"Onion weather?" Tony repeated, not understanding what she meant.

She giggled. "Well, you feel like an onion when you have to wear so many layers of clothing! But never mind," she went on, "I've got something pretty underneath." She quickly stripped off the wet raincoat and cloak to reveal an elegant, dark red velvet dress with

a stand-up collar.

"Brilliant!" said Tony, impressed.

"My clothes aren't bad either!" growled the Little Vampire, as he too shed his raincoat and cloak. To his amazement, Tony saw that Rudolph was dressed in black knee breeches, a black dinner jacket and a mauve shirt with a ruffle down the front.

"Where did you get your outfits from?" he asked.

The Little Vampire threw Anna a gloating look. "The clothes are from her 'ex'!"

"Pig!" spat Anna.

"Didn't these things come from Igno von Rant, then?" asked the Little Vampire innocently.

"Yes, they did!" Anna admitted through clenched teeth. "But he is *not* my 'ex'! Quite the contrary – I think he was mean and revolting!"

"That's new!"

"It certainly isn't! What's more, for a start it was *he* who tried to get friendly with me, and not the other way round. And secondly, how was I supposed to know that he was really a Professor Careless, doing research into vampires? And thirdly," continued Anna in a louder voice, "you're only saying all this because you want to spoil the Christmas spirit for Tony and me!"

"I do hope you don't," Tony's father put in. Tony whipped round with a start. He had completely forgotten about his parents!

They were standing at the other end of the hall. They probably hadn't wanted to interrupt while the children were saying hello, and were now looking at them expectantly. Tony wondered uneasily how long they'd been standing there, and how much of the conversation they'd overheard.

"Aren't you going to ask your friends in?" suggested

Tony's dad.

To cover up his confusion, Tony stepped to one side and said in a particularly jolly voice, "Come on in, as long as you aren't vamp—" He'd been about to say "vampires", but stopped himself just in time.

"Vampire researchers!" Anna finished with a giggle.

Rudolph dug her in the ribs and hissed, "Have you forgotten what we agreed?"

"No," said Anna, looking guilty.

"What have you agreed?" asked Tony's father nosily.

"Oh, nothing much," replied the Little Vampire. "Just family business."

He went over to Tony's mother, held out his hand and, with a deep bow, said, "Happy Christmas, Mrs Peasbody. And many thanks for inviting us."

Then he shook Tony's father by the hand. "Happy Christmas, Mr Peasbody. Many thanks for inviting us!" he said.

"Once would have been enough!" laughed Dad, looking rather surprised, Tony thought.

"Our family motto is: 'Better too much at once than too little'!" Anna remarked, bursting out laughing.

"Sssh!" The Little Vampire hissed.

"Why don't you hang up your wet things in the bathroom?" suggested Tony's mum, pointing to the cloaks and raincoats that were draped over Anna and Rudolph's arms. Damp patches had already formed on the carpet.

"In the bathroom?" The Little Vampire stared at her in shocked surprise. "No way!"

"But they'll have to dry out," explained Tony's mother.

Tony was just worrying that she might want to take a closer look at the cloaks, when Anna said, "We'll hang them up in Tony's room!" and marched firmly off to his bedroom.

"Yes, that's what we'll do," cried Rudolph, following her.

Tony wanted to run after them, but his father held him by the sleeve. "At least take the bowl from the bathroom to put under the cloaks."

"This Christmas Eve is going to be full of surprises, I can see!" Tony's mother sighed. "I think Dad and I will go and light the candles. We'll ring the bell when we're ready."

I'm So Excited!

When Tony reached his room, he saw to his horror that Rudolph and Anna were bouncing about on his bed as though it were a trampoline.

"Oh, I'm so excited! So excited!" sang Anna at the top of her voice as the Little Vampire clapped his hands in time.

"Have you gone mad?" called Tony.

"Yes!" laughed Anna. "We're madly excited!" And she began to trill once more, "Oh, I'm so excited! So excited! So excited!" This time the Little Vampire joined in too.

Furious, Tony dumped the bowl on the floor and threw the wet raincoats, which were lying in a heap by the cupboard, into it.

"Hey, be a bit more careful!" barked the Little Vampire. "Do you want our precious raincoats to tear?"

"No," growled Tony. "But I do want you to get off my bed."

Anna sprang off the bed in one bound. "You must be out of your tinselly – oops, I mean tiny – mind!" she teased.

"What do you mean?"

"Tinselly mind! I sound just like Sniveller!" Anna said, laughing uproariously. "Greg said that all the rush and bustle of Christmas had been too much for Sniveller's nerves. When he rang him up, he answered the telephone saying, 'Snookery here – er, no, I mean McSnivell!' " Rudolph and Anna doubled up with laughter. Even Tony couldn't help joining in.

"You're not cross any more, are you?" Anna asked him tenderly.

"Me?" Tony blushed, turning away quickly and pointing to the wet patch in front of his cupboard. "I was cross because you'd chucked your raincoats on the floor and were jumping about on my bed!" he explained.

"But it's Christmas – my very first Christmas!" cried Anna with sparkling eyes, hopping about on the spot. "I'm so happy and I've just *got* to let it out!"

Tony cleared his throat. "Actually, Christmas ought to be a peaceful time."

"Peaceful?" said Anna, puzzled.

"That's what my parents say. I'm sure they won't want us to make all this noise, especially if we might disturb the neighbours."

"But I'm *so* excited!" Anna said looking at him pleadingly. "Couldn't I just bounce for a little bit more – just five minutes?"

"No!" answered the Little Vampire gruffly. "You heard what Tony said. Anyway, you don't have to keep fidgeting about like a baby!"

Anna put on a pained expression. "You were doing it too!" The Little Vampire turned his head away and kept a dignified silence.

"Don't fight, you two!" pleaded Tony.

"Huh! *I* wasn't fighting!" retorted Anna. "Rudolph's the one who keeps on being annoying!"

"What, me?" snapped the Little Vampire. "*You* started it!"

"Sssh!" whispered Tony imploringly, pointing to the door. "You could put a bit more powder on," he suggested to Anna. "Your make-up's rather smudged."

"Is it?" said Anna. "That must have been the rain!"

"Well, I don't feel like making my face all dusty again," announced the Little Vampire, staring at Tony. "Unless . . ."

"Unless what?" asked Tony uneasily.

"Unless people can tell that I'm . . . a vampire otherwise!" he finished.

"No, no!" Tony reassured him. "You just look rather brightly coloured, but not at all like vampires!"

"It's nice to look brightly coloured," said the Little Vampire with his grating laugh. "We'll match the presents and the brightly coloured wrapping paper!"

Anna drew herself up. "I don't want to look brightly coloured! But I haven't brought any powder with me," she said, turning to Tony. She picked up a black bag which lay half-hidden under the bed and which Tony hadn't noticed before. "I've got your presents in here," she explained.

"I can fetch some powder from the bathroom," Tony offered.

Anna nodded her thanks. "And a hairbrush too, please!" she said.

"What about a lipstick?" suggested the Little Vampire.

"Do you want to put on some more lipstick?" asked Tony in surprise.

"Me? No!" Rudolph grinned. "But I'm sure Anna wants to make herself some kissable lips!"

"Creep!" spat Anna, going redder and redder.

"What do you mean?" Rudolph pretended to be innocent. "Didn't you say on the way here that you were going to give Tony a Christmas kiss?"

"I'll – I'll go and get the powder," said Tony quickly, moving towards the door but just then, a bright tinkling sound could be heard.

"Too late," he said to Anna. "That's the Christmas bell."

"Am I going to get my presents now?" asked the Little Vampire in his throaty voice.

"We," Anna corrected him. "*We* will be getting *our* presents!"

"I hope not!" retorted the Little Vampire. "I don't think much of any present I have to share with you!"

The bell rang for a second time. Tony went over to his desk and picked up the bag containing the Christmas presents he had bought and made. "Let's go," he said.

The Little Vampire grabbed hold of the black bag and called out, "Off to the coffins, ready, steady, go!"

What A Christmas Tree

The Little Vampire stopped in front of the living room door. "After you," he said to Tony, with a grin.

Tony opened the door and was almost dazzled for a moment. He knew his parents had bought a particularly tall, bushy Christmas tree, but now he saw it in all its magnificence, with lighted candles and all the Christmas decorations.

"How beautiful!" exclaimed Anna, and the Little Vampire croaked, "You've sure got a mega-tree there!"

"Do you like it?" Tony's mum was smiling and looking pleased with herself.

"Yes!" breathed Anna, adding, "Our Christmas trees are horrible."

"Do you mean you've got more than one Christmas tree?" asked Dad in surprise.

"Yes, nine," answered Anna.

Tony's mother pricked up her ears. "Nine? Why so many?"

"Greg got hold of them all," explained Anna.

"Greg . . ." Tony's mother had gone pale. "Do you know by any chance where he got them from?" she asked, holding back her excitement with difficulty.

"No," replied Anna.

"I do!" the Little Vampire chuckled. "He just helped a Christmas-tree seller unload his stock!"

"Oh, so that's it—" Tony's mother sighed in relief.

"Tony told us you wouldn't be celebrating Christmas," remarked Dad.

"We don't," the Little Vampire agreed. "But this year we wanted to make it look a bit more festive in the vault—" He broke off and whipped his hand to his mouth in confusion.

"Vault?" repeated Tony's father merrily. "That sounds like something out of a vampire film!"

"Doesn't it?" said Anna. "Rudolph really has been watching too many vampire films!" She winked at Tony and giggled.

"Oh, look! It's my Olga!" the Little Vampire exclaimed suddenly, walking up to the tree with a glazed expression on his face and gazing at the dangling Christmas angels.

"You can choose one for yourself later on," declared Tony quickly. "That'd be all right, Mum, wouldn't it?"

His mother nodded. "Of course!"

"We haven't got any decorations at all," said Anna, touching the fragile glass figures carefully.

"No decorations at all – for nine trees?" Dad sounded astonished. "Would you like to take a few bells and balls away as well?"

Anna shook her head. "I don't think we'd be allowed to hang them up."

"You don't have it very easy at home, do you?" said Mum, looking sympathetically from Anna to Rudolph and back again.

"Oh, you know, our family doesn't have it very easy with us sometimes," answered Rudolph. "Especially not with my little sister!"

"Me?" exclaimed Anna indignantly. "Huh! I'm an elected member of the Family Council!"

"But apart from that, you're not much of an

advertisement for our family, are you?" remarked the Little Vampire with a spiteful grin.

Anna clenched her fists and hissed, "You mean beast!"

"Please don't fight!" said Tony.

"That's right, no fighting on Christmas Eve," his mother agreed. "Anyway, we ought to be getting on with giving out the Christmas presents!"

"At last!" exclaimed the Little Vampire.

Tony's mother went over to the record player and put on some Christmas carols. A choir of children started to sing "Away in a Manger".

Anna listened with a rapt expression on her face. "Music . . . we love music!"

"Sshh!" the Little Vampire whispered warningly.

"Would you like to sing us a carol, Anna?" asked Tony's dad.

"Me?" she repeated, sounding confused.

"Yes." He switched the record player off. "After all, it's much nicer to sing ourselves. Our son only ever listens to records," he went on. "Even though his school report says he's got a very good voice."

"Tony? A good voice?" exclaimed the Little Vampire with a laugh.

"He never sings at home, more's the pity!" said Tony's mother, with a disapproving look in the direction of the Little Vampire.

"Yes, because my vocal cords get stretched quite enough while I'm at school!" countered Tony grimly.

"Now," said Tony's father, nodding encouragingly at Anna. "How would you like to sing us a carol? What about 'Silent Night'?"

"I—" Anna plucked at a strand of hair. "I don't know the words – I mean, I've forgotten them," she added. "But I do know a Christmas poem," she said, after a pause.

"Oh, a poem!" Tony's mother sounded very pleased. Anna stood on tiptoe.

"Christmas is a lovely time.
Then I'm never lonely.
While outside the bells do chime
I'm here with my friend Tony."

"*Your* friend Tony?" growled the Little Vampire. "*Our* friend Tony, if you don't mind!"

"*Our?*" Anna pretended not to get the point. "Didn't you say earlier on that you didn't think much of any present we had to share?" She giggled, but quickly put a hand to her mouth. Tony's parents looked at one another in surprise.

"Well, you all seem to know each other very well indeed," remarked Mum.

"I wouldn't say *very* well," replied Anna. "But another old vam— I mean, family saying of ours is: 'All things come in their own good time'!"

"Well, anyway, you seem to know each other better than anyone would realize from what Tony tells us," said Mum.

"What does Tony tell you, then?" asked the Little Vampire.

"Hardly anything – that's why we're so surprised," explained Dad.

Anna smiled craftily. "Mmm, on the one hand, it's obviously not very flattering to us that he doesn't tell you aything . . ."

"But on the other hand, it's quite understandable," the Little Vampire finished for her. He winked at Anna, and the two began to laugh happily – this time in total agreement.

104

High Time to Open Presents

Tony's mother cleared her throat. "I think it really is time to open the presents now," she said, trying to hold on to her composure.

"High time, I'd say!" croaked the Little Vampire. "Where are the presents?"

"There, where they always are," answered Dad. "Under the Christmas tree." He switched on the lamp by the sofa.

Anna gave a cry. "The light – it's so bright!"

"Hey, pull yourself together!" the Little Vampire hissed.

"But it was much gloomier and tombier with the candles!" retorted Anna.

"Gloomier and tombier?" repeated Tony's father, sounding amused.

"Anna meant dim and shadowy," explained Rudolph. "My little sister often lets the cat out of the bag."

"What do you mean, 'lets the cat out of the bag'?" asked Tony's mother, looking searchingly from Rudolph to Anna.

"What do I mean?" The Little Vampire scratched his chin, obviously at a loss for an answer.

"Yes. What is it that Anna's not supposed to talk about?" probed Tony's mother.

"Oh, I see what you mean." The Little Vampire

tapped his forehead knowingly. "I didn't mean she lets the cat out of the bag – I meant she can't always find the right words and expressions, you see!"

"Just like you!" snorted Anna.

"But I'm sure she'll be able to find the right presents!" said Tony's father, laughing kindly. "Would you like to start, Anna?"

"Yes, please," answered Anna, bending over the packages. After a short search, she got up, reddening, and said, "This one says, 'For Anna'."

Tony immediately recognized the parcel containing the make-up. Anna ran her hands solemnly over the brightly coloured wrapping paper, decorated with teddy bears.

"If it's got your name on it, you can open it," Tony's dad said encouragingly.

Anna smiled, suddenly unusually shy. She carried the package over to the table and began to untie the red string carefully.

The Little Vampire rocked impatiently on tiptoe. "Hurry up!" he hissed. "There are other people waiting to open their presents too!"

"You don't have to wait till Anna's finished opening hers," said Tony's mum.

"Don't I?" cried the Little Vampire.

"No," she assured him. "We're not as strict as that here."

Now there was no stopping the Little Vampire. He threw himself on the presents and, unlike Anna, came back to the table with a whole armful.

"All for me!" he announced proudly.

"All of them?" said Tony doubtfully. Had they really bought that many for the Little Vampire? Six – no, seven – different parcels and little packages were laid out in front of him.

106

Of course, he opened the biggest one first, "Oh, only a box of matches!" he exclaimed in disappointment.

"It's a special family pack," explained Tony. "To keep you going for half a century!"

The Little Vampire looked doubtful. "I thought Christmas was the time for *personal* gifts," he hissed.

"Yes it is," Tony's father agreed. "If I were you, I'd look in the other parcels."

Rudolph muttered something unintelligible and began to unwrap the smallest package.

"A lighter! How original!" he said scornfully. His mood got worse when he found a torch in the third package.

Tony's mother gave an embarrassed laugh, as though she had chosen all the presents herself. "Tony thought you'd both find these things very useful," she said.

"Both?" The Little Vampire gave Tony a scathing look. "So I've got to share these presents!"

Tony shrugged. "If I had known you wouldn't be pleased with them, I'd have saved my money!" he retorted.

"*I'm* pleased, though," Anna put in. "I'm ever so pleased with mine!" She held up the make-up bag, lipstick and powder compact with shining eyes. "These presents are really great!" She gave a little sniff of emotion.

"Do open the blue parcel!" Tony's mother suggested to the Little Vampire.

The vampire opened the package unenthusiastically, then cried out in surprise. On the outside of the box was the word "Walkman".

"Walkman? *Walkman*? I *hate* walking!" he muttered.

Tony found it hard to keep a straight face. " 'Walkman' means a personal stereo – you can listen to music while you're walking around."

"Really?" exclaimed the Little Vampire. "And . . . flying?"

"Yes, it will work in a plane," Tony's mother told him.

The Little Vampire had gone quite pink with pleasure and excitement. "For listening to music . . ." he said, carefully lifting the equipment out of its box.

"What's this for?" he asked, pointing to the headphones.

"You have to put those on," explained Dad.

"Put them on? Where?"

"Over your ears, of course!"

"Then what?"

"Then you press the button marked 'Play', and you'll hear music!"

Anna had moved over next to Rudolph and was eyeing the Walkman curiously. "I've often seen those," she said, "but only in shop windows."

"Only in shop windows?" repeated Mum. "Won't your parents let you have a Walkman?" She looked over at Tony in surprise. "Is it like mirrors?"

"Mirrors?" Anna took a step backwards.

"Yes. Tony told us your parents won't allow mirrors in the house for ideological reasons."

"Idiotical reasons?" Anna winked at Rudolph and they began to giggle, as if on cue.

"Isn't it true?" asked Mum.

"Yes, yes," said the Little Vampire. "You know, we aren't much like other people."

Tony's mother waved her hands distractedly. "Then . . . then perhaps the powder and lipstick aren't very suitable presents."

"Oh, they're very suitable!" Anna assured her. "I'd love to try them out – in the bathroom, if that's all right with you."

"Why not?" answered Tony's mother.

Anna ran over to the door. "Won't be a minute!" she called.

The Most Difficult Part of the Evening

In the meantime, the Little Vampire had put on the headphones and pressed the "Play" button several times without success.

"You have to put a cassette in first!" Tony explained.

"What did you say?" growled the Little Vampire.

"Take the headphones off, then you'll hear!" Tony bellowed.

Rudolph did so. "The stupid thing won't work," he announced.

"I don't think that's very polite," Tony's father reproached him. "Don't you think you're jumping to conclusions?"

"What do you mean? The silly thing won't make a sound!" replied the Little Vampire, handing the Walkman to Tony's father. "Listen yourself!"

Without a word, Tony's father went over to the music shelves, picked out a cassette and put it in the Walkman.

"Here. Perhaps you should try it again," he said in a gently scornful voice, "before you write the machine off completely."

The Little Vampire put the headphones back on and, looking bored with the whole thing, pressed "Play" once more. Even Tony could hear the music – he obviously had the volume turned right up.

The Little Vampire began to grin. Then his expression

changed: beads of sweat appeared on his forehead, his lips trembled – and suddenly he ripped the headphones off with a cry of rage.

"What is it now?" asked Dad.

"Rummage!" groaned the Little Vampire. "It's Doctor Rummage!"

"Which cassette did you put in?" asked Tony with a feeling of dread. "It wasn't the one we got from Nether Bogsbottom, was it?"

His father nodded. "But what's Rudolph got against 'The Merry Village Warblers' with Ernest Albert Rummage?"

"He . . . he doesn't like folk music," said Tony quickly.

There were still beads of sweat on the Little Vampire's forehead. He must be remembering the holiday they had had on the farm, and how the village doctor, Doctor Rummage, who hunted vampires in his spare time, had almost caught him. Tony had only managed to save him at the last minute.

"You can get some really good cassettes, you know," Tony assured him, to take his mind off it. He pointed to the presents. "If I were you, I'd have a look at the red parcel."

Rudolph grabbed the package and unwrapped the two pop cassettes Tony had bought. The Little Vampire studied the labels suspiciously. Finally he said, "Hmm, they sound all right," and pushed one of them into his Walkman. He listened and then – at long last – he smiled.

Moving his head and shoulders in time to the music, he set about opening the rest of his presents. The music seemed to have put him in a better mood, because even the candles that Tony had chosen for him brought a friendly smile to his face. And when he saw *Sixteen Black Tales for Those Who Love the Dark*, he nodded appreciatively at Tony.

"Thank goodness for that!" Tony's mother whispered to his father. "We seem to have got the most difficult part of the evening behind us!"

"Hallo!" said Anna suddenly. She was standing in the doorway, and had put so much powder on that her face looked quite peculiar, like a mask. She had painted her lips quite neatly but hadn't done her bright red cheeks so well.

Tony had to grin, and even his parents chuckled. "Don't you think I look nice?" asked Anna, glancing uncertainly from one to the other.

"Well," said Tony's mother diplomatically, "considering that you're never allowed to look in a mirror . . ."

"The powder's too thick," explained Tony. He knew Anna hated people who lied to be kind.

She giggled with embarrassment. "The brush felt so nice and tickly – I just put on more and more!" She went up to Tony's parents, shook hands with them, curtsied, and said, "Thank you very much for the presents!"

"You haven't opened them all yet," Tony told her.

"Yes, look under the Christmas tree," added Mum, obviously impressed by Anna's "good manners". Anna bent down. Then she came back to the table with three presents. Tony and his parents watched her unpack the red candles, the diary with the silver key, and her book, *The Best Vampire Love Stories*.

By the time Anna had finished, there were tears in her eyes. "So many things . . ." she whispered. And before Tony knew what was happening, Anna had flung her arms round his neck and had kissed him on both cheeks.

"Thank you, Tony!" she whispered.

"What for?" he asked evasively.

"For everything," she replied, "but especially for the book." She ran her fingers over the dark blue cover. "I never knew such a book existed . . . vampire love stories!"

It Belonged to Our Family

"Have you read it already?" she asked after a moment, looking expectantly at Tony.

"Of course not!" he answered indignantly. "You shouldn't read books you're going to give as presents!"

"Oh really?" said Mum. "What about Rudolph's book?"

She pointed over at the sofa, where the Little Vampire – his headphones still over his ears – was deep in *Sixteen Black Stories*.

"I only tried out Rudolph's book," explained Tony. "After all, Anna and Rudolph don't read any old vampire stories!"

"That's right!" Anna said. "We don't read violent stories or ones which only show vampires in a bad light."

Tony's father laughed. "You're choosy, aren't you?"

"Of course," she agreed. "We've got very particular tastes, haven't we, Tony?"

With a giggle, Anna ran over to the old black bag she'd left by the door. Almost immediately, she was back with two presents wrapped in crumpled tissue paper.

"I hope this is to *your* taste!" she said, giving one package to Tony's mother. "And that this is to *your* taste!" she smiled to Tony, holding out the other one.

Tony hesitated before opening the parcel, but then his mother gave a cry of surprise: "Oh, look! A candlestick!"

"What a magnificent piece!" added Dad.

"It belonged to our family," Anna revealed.

"Magnificent" wasn't the word Tony would have used: "ancient" was more like it.

"It's a real antique," remarked Tony's mother.

"About twenty years old, I'd guess," said Dad.

"Oh, it's much older than that," Anna corrected him. "It dates from 1848."

"As old as that?" whistled Tony's father. "Isn't it rather valuable?"

"Yes, Anna – we can't accept such a valuable present," said Mum.

"Yes, you can," Anna smiled. "Firstly, it's from both of us – Rudolph and me. Secondly, it was so kind of you to invite us here – the candlestick's nothing in comparison."

"What about your parents?" asked Dad. "Did they agree to this? I mean, the candlestick used to belong to your family."

Anna winked at Tony. "It'll probably be staying in the family, after all . . ."

Tony blushed and quickly turned to his present. It was a small black cushion, embroidered all over with beads. He could make out a dark red heart with two entwined letters in black: "A" for Anna and "T" for Tony.

"I made it for you myself," whispered Anna tenderly.

"Did you?" said Tony. "It must have taken weeks!"

"My grandmother did help me a little," Anna admitted, "but I thought up the pattern myself. Do you like it?"

Tony nodded. "It's very artistic."

"Do you think so?" Anna smiled and looked pleased. "What else?" she asked.

"What do you mean?" said Tony.

"Well, what else do you think about it?"

Tony looked at his parents. As he might have known,

they were following every word with rapt attention. What a pity they weren't wearing headphones like the Little Vampire!

"Well, I think the cushion's brilliant," he said. "It'll go in the place of honour."

"On your bed?" asked Anna, expectantly. She obviously didn't care that his parents were standing close by with ears pricked!

Tony coughed with embarrassment. "I – I don't know," he said.

"But that's what I made it for," Anna told him. "After all, I want you to have sweet dreams!"

Tony could have insisted that he would probably be more likely to get nightmares from the stink of decay streaming from the cushion. But he didn't want to hurt Anna, so he said, "I'll have to try it out."

"Yes, you must," she giggled. "Then all the wishes I've sewn into it will come true!"

"What sort of wishes?" asked Tony's father, not very tactfully.

"Oh—" Anna sounded puzzled. "Lots of different ones – one for each bead."

"Then Tony will be a lucky chap!" Dad laughed. "I bet there are at least two hundred beads on there!"

"Three hundred," Anna told him. "Three hundred and thirty-three, to be exact."

"And you've made that many wishes for Tony?"

"Yes," Anna said, gazing solemnly at Tony. "You should never have to choose between wishes," she went on. "And most important of all, you must always believe they'll come true!"

As she spoke, Tony felt a shiver run down his spine. "I . . . I still haven't looked at what *you've* given me!" he said, turning hastily to his parents.

Goose à la Peasbody

"And I haven't looked at the dinner!" his mother put in, rushing to the door.

"Oh, no! I hope nothing awful has happened," said Dad, running after her.

Suddenly Anna and Tony found themselves alone – apart from the Little Vampire. He was sitting on the sofa, twitching in time to the music, not taking the slightest notice of what was going on around him.

"Shall I tell you what wishes I sewed into your present?" asked Anna softly.

Tony cleared his throat. "I . . . I don't think this is the right moment," he replied.

"Why not?" asked Anna, rather hurt.

"Because my parents will be back at any moment," he replied, "with our Christmas goose."

The corners of Anna's mouth turned down in disgust.

"It'll taste delicious!" Tony assured her. "At any rate, I think it will," he added.

"Not this Christmas, I'm afraid!" Tony's father was back in the living room, looking very upset. "The goose has burned – what a shame!"

"Burned?" exclaimed Tony indignantly. He'd been looking forward all year to the Christmas goose with its tasty stuffing of nuts, apples and raisins.

His father shrugged his shoulders unhappily. "We were all too busy with other things . . ." He smiled

118

apologetically at Anna. "But when you spend Christmas Eve with such charming guests, it's easy to forget the goose in the oven! Luckily we've still got dessert," he went on soothingly. "It's a red one."

"And the goose is only burned on the outside," added Tony's mother, who had just come in carrying a tray of dishes.

She began to lay the table. Tony's father helped her and in the twinkling of an eye, they had transformed the table into a festive-looking spread.

Anna gazed in rapture at the china painted with roses, the silver cutlery and the starched white table napkins. When Tony's mother placed the candlestick from Anna and Rudolph in the middle of the table, and fixed a red candle in it, Anna sighed contentedly. "This is just how I imagined Christmas would be," she said.

"I do hope you won't be too disappointed with the food," remarked Dad.

"I don't think so," said Anna lightly.

"Then I'll go and fetch the goose," announced Tony's mother. "Or rather, I'll fetch what's left of it!"

The goose wasn't as charred as Tony had feared. His parents must have cut off the skin, but the meat and the stuffing looked as appetising as ever. Suddenly he realized he felt extremely hungry. His parents seemed to feel the same.

"Let's sit down," said Tony's father, looking encouragingly at the Little Vampire. But Rudolph didn't react.

"Hey!" Anna tapped him on the shoulder. "Tony's parents want to eat now!"

"What is it?" growled the Little Vampire.

"It's dinner time!" cried Anna.

"I can't hear you!" thundered the Little Vampire.

Anna snatched the headphones off his head, and before Rudolph could protest she said warningly, "Just remember what we agreed!"

"All right!" hissed the Little Vampire, and surprisingly obedient, came and sat down at the table.

"You're making us very curious with all these agreements of yours!" Tony's father laughed.

"Oh, it was just to be on the safe side," said Anna.

"On the safe side?" repeated Tony's mother.

"Yes, so we didn't upset anything," explained Anna, "since we're . . . so unused to celebrating Christmas."

"I'm sure you won't be unused to eating!" joked Tony's father, laying slices of meat on Anna and Rudolph's plates. "Tuck in!" he said. "We hope you like our Christmas goose, in spite of everything."

He could have saved his breath, because the Little Vampire suddenly gave a cry and held his hands to his tummy.

"Have you got a pain?" inquired Tony's mother, anxiously.

"Oh, my tummy!" groaned the Little Vampire.

"Is it because you're hungry?" asked Mum.

"No!" moaned the vampire. "It's because of the goose!"

"But your sister likes goose," Tony's father said smiling, trying to keep calm.

"Did she say that?" The Little Vampire looked at Anna darkly out of the corner of his eye.

"Well, not exactly," admitted Dad.

"Rudolph's unhappy because of the goose," Anna explained. "He loves animals, you see. Don't you, Rudolph?" she said, looking at him imploringly.

The Little Vampire muttered something no one could catch.

"He` shouldn't feel sorry for the goose," declared Tony's mother. "It was a very old bird."

"I *am* sorry for it, though," retorted the Little Vampire, biting his lip. "It can't fly any. more, poor goose. And it's *so* lovely to be able to fly!"

Tony's parents looked at each other, rather at a loss.

"Are you both vegetarians?" asked Tony's mother after a pause.

"Hedge barbarians?" The Little Vampire gave a throaty chuckle. "I suppose you *could* say we're hedge barbarians!" He nudged Anna, who was sitting next to him. "What do you think?"

Anna sat up. "The fact is, we don't eat meat, Mrs Peasbody," she said with dignity.

Tony's mother gave an embarrassed smile. "Then perhaps we'd better go straight on to dessert . . ."

At that moment, there was a ring at the door.

Ready For My Coffin

"Who can that be?" asked Tony's mother in surprise.

"Probably Granny and Grandpa," said Tony.

"No," she shook her head. "They're not coming till tomorrow."

"I expect it's Father Christmas himself!" joked Dad, getting up.

"Or Mrs Grumpson, come to complain yet again!" Tony's mother said, following him with a sigh.

"Do you think it's Mrs Grumpson?" asked Anna in a whisper, when they were alone.

Tony grinned. "Mr or Mrs . . . they'll be in a grump, whoever it is!" But the grin left his face when he heard a voice saying "Happy Christmas!" – a voice that alternated between high and squeaky and deep and husky.

"G-Greg!" stammered the Little Vampire.

"Oh, Dracula! No . . ." said Anna.

Footsteps thumped down the hall, and then Greg was peering into the room. "Aha! So there you are," he said. "But what long faces!" He laughed menacingly. "Has Father Christmas forgotten you? Well, never mind – now you've got me instead!"

"Worse luck!" complained Anna.

"Worse luck?" Greg sounded hurt. "Do you mean I'm not welcome?"

"No, no," Tony's mother assured him. She was

standing in the doorway with Tony's father. "Of course you're welcome – just as welcome as Anna and Rudolph."

"Thank you," said Greg. "That's just what we like to hear." With a loud groan, he flopped down on the chair that Tony's father had been sitting on earlier. "At last a chance to sit down!" he said in relief.

"Hasn't McRookery got any chairs then?" asked Tony spitefully.

"Very funny!" growled Greg. "How would *you* like to stand to attention for half an hour in front of a Christmas tree singing carols – especially when the whole place stinks of garlic? Yuk!"

"It can't have been as bad as that," said Anna. "We've been standing by Tony's Christmas tree too."

"But we haven't been singing," Tony's father put in.

"Anyway, you haven't heard the half of it yet!" Greg went on self-importantly. "After the singing, we were at last going to sit down when McRookery had this . . . this attack, and I had to support him till the ambulance arrived!"

"McRookery had an attack?" exclaimed the Little Vampire. "Do you mean another heart attack?"

"No," answered Greg dully. "A fainting fit. And I would have had one too if I hadn't found this chair in the nick of time." He ran a hand over his forehead. "Now I really do feel ready for my coffin!"

"For your coffin?" repeated Tony's mother. "You shouldn't joke about such things, especially not on Christmas Eve."

"Exactly!" Anna giggled. "You shouldn't joke about these things." She winked at the Little Vampire and Rudolph began to giggle as well.

Tony's mother looked at Anna and Rudolph reprovingly, but didn't say anything.

"Would you like something to get your strength up?" she asked Greg.

"Get my strength up? Oh, yes please!" cried Greg huskily, running his tongue quickly over his lips. Looking greedily at Tony's mother's neck, he said, "It needn't be much – just a little drop would work wonders . . ."

"A little drop?" exclaimed Anna hotly. "Are you out of your mind?"

"No, what do you mean?" replied Greg. His eyes had already begun to get that fixed vampire look. "She was offering it herself . . ."

"Let's go!" said Anna firmly. "Come on Rudolph – help me!" She had jumped up and taken hold of Greg's right arm. "Take the other side."

"No, I'll carry the bag," replied the Little Vampire, adding maliciously, "After all, *I* don't care to get into trouble with Greg!"

"And you don't care about the Peasbody family either, do you?" hissed Anna, pushing Greg past Tony's parents and out into the hall. Greg, who was acting strangely stiff and vacant, put up no resistance.

"I . . . I don't understnad," said Tony's mum. "You mustn't all leave! There's plenty of food here for Greg. And if he doesn't like goose either, I'm sure Tony would give up his dessert—"

"Another time," Anna said shortly. Turning to the Little Vampire, she whispered, "Quick! Get our raincoats and cloaks from Tony's room!"

"W-wait a minute!" answered the Little Vampire. He had opened the bag and taken out a fat package wrapped in brown paper. "Here," he said to Tony. "I almost forgot: here's your Christmas present."

"Thank you," said Tony in surprise.

He watched as Rudolph stowed away the Walkman, the book and all the other presents, including Anna's, in the black leather bag. Then the Little Vampire ran into Tony's room and came back with the two raincoats and cloaks.

"Hurry!" Anna urged him. "Greg's coming round!"

"But . . ." Tony's mother stammered, but the three vampires were already out of the flat.

Tony hastily closed the door behind them. You never knew what a starving, disappointed Greg might be capable of . . .

When Tony got back to the living room, his parents were sitting on the sofa looking rather exhausted.

"What a Christmas Eve!" sighed Mum.

"At least it was different," said Tony's dad, still trying to make jokes.

"More like a strange encounter of the third kind!" said Mum.

"Third kind?" Tony pretended not to understand.

"Well, that's what that vampire film at the cinema was called."

"Vampire film?" Tony shook his head. "Science fiction film, you mean."

"Oh, it's all the same totally unrealistic thing," she said. "Miles from reality."

"If you say so . . ." Tony grinned, starting to unwrap the package Rudolph had given him.

When he had opened the parcel Tony couldn't believe his eyes. It contained his own books – all the ones Rudolph had ever "borrowed" from him. The only one still missing was the newest, *Vampires by Themselves*.

"What an original present!" remarked Mum. She had of course recognized all the books at once.

"Well, a very surprising one, anyway," said Tony.

His mother stood up. "I'm going to make a cup of tea," she announced. "And then we'll start all over again and celebrate *our* Christmas this time!"

It turned into a very peaceful evening: much too peaceful, Tony thought. But at least he got the red anorak he'd wanted so much, as well as a thick book called *Sinister Tales from Scotland*, a new tracksuit and a game. And an added bonus was that he got three helpings of dessert: Anna's, Rudolph's and his own!

Find out what happens to Tony and his vampire friends in the next book in this series, *The Little Vampire and the Castle of Count Dracula*.

THE LITTLE VAMPIRE SERIES

Watch out for new titles in the Little Vampire series:

These books can be bought or ordered from your local bookshop. For more information about these and other good books, contact *The Sales Department, Simon & Schuster Young Books, Campus 400, Maylands Avenue, Hemel Hempstead, Herts HP2 7EZ.*